Schoolhouse Phonics

Level B

CONTENTS

Circle the letters in each box that go together.

1.	2.	3.	4.
A k B a	W w L I	G n N h	L m M n
5.	**6.**	**7.**	**8.**
O v V o	C c G g	H p P w	Z f E z
9.	**10.**	**11.**	**12.**
T d D t	F w U f	X j J x	R r E e
13.	**14.**	**15.**	**16.**
S y Y s	K x V k	H j I i	Q b B q

Write the capital and small letters of the alphabet in the correct order.

Aa   Bb

Nn

Yy

Write the letter that comes before.

__ c __ d	__ __ q	__ __ n	__ __ f
__ __ p	__ __ g	__ __ r	__ __ t
__ __ z	__ __ s	__ __ u	__ __ e
__ __ h	__ __ l	__ __ b	__ __ w
__ __ v	__ __ f	__ __ j	__ __ i

Write the letter that comes next.

b __ c __	g __ __	f __ __	a __ __
k __ __	q __ __	v __ __	l __ __
m __ __	j __ __	p __ __	e __ __
c __ __	s __ __	u __ __	r __ __
h __ __	d __ __	x __ __	i __ __

Write the missing letters in each group of four letters.

a b c d	k _ m _	h i _ _
q _ s _	e _ _ h	j _ _ m
_ g _ i	_ n o _	_ s t _
w _ _ z	_ p q _	w x _ _
_ e f _	b _ d _	_ c d _
l _ _ o	_ j _ l	_ _ v w
u _ w _	_ s t _	d e _ _
k l _ _	u _ w _	n _ _ q
_ t _ v	_ g h _	_ f _ h
c _ e _	r _ _ u	_ _ l m

Say each picture name. Write the letter that stands for the beginning consonant sound.

1. ___ S ___	**2.** _____	**3.** _____	**4.** _____
5. _____	**6.** _____	**7.** _____	**8.** _____
9. _____	**10.** _____	**11.** _____	**12.** _____
13. _____	**14.** _____	**15.** _____	**16.** _____

Initial consonants **s, m, t, p, n, r, b,** and **j**   Unit 2/Lesson 3   **7**

Say each picture name. Write the letter that stands for the ending consonant sound.

1.

_____
t

2.

_____

_____

3.

_____

_____

4.

_____

_____

5.

_____

_____

6.

_____

_____

7.

_____

_____

8.

_____

_____

9.

_____

_____

10.

_____

_____

11.

_____

_____

12.

_____

_____

13.

_____

_____

14.

_____

_____

15.

_____

_____

16.

_____

_____

Final consonants **s, m, t, p, n, r,** and **b**

Say each picture name. Write the letter that stands for the beginning consonant sound.

1. f	**2.** _____	**3.** _____	**4.** _____
5. _____	**6.** _____	**7.** _____	**8.** _____
9. _____	**10.** _____	**11.** _____	**12.** _____
13. _____	**14.** _____	**15.** _____	**16.** _____

Inital consonants **f, d, l, h, w, k, y, v,** and **z**   Unit 2/Lesson 4   **9**

Say each picture name. Write the letter that stands for the ending consonant sound.

1.

k

2.

___

3.

___

4.

___

5.

___

6.

___

7.

___

8.

___

9.

___

10.

___

11.

___

12.

___

13.

___

14.

___

15.

___

16.

___

Say each picture name. Write the letter that stands for the consonant sound you hear in the middle of the word.

1.	2.	3.	4.
g _____	_____	_____	_____
_____	_____	_____	_____

5.	6.	7.	8.
_____	_____	_____	_____
_____	_____	_____	_____

9.	10.	11.	12.
_____	_____	_____	_____
_____	_____	_____	_____

13.	14.	15.	16.
_____	_____	_____	_____
_____	_____	_____	_____

Medial consonants **d, b, l, t, m, p, v, g, n,** and **k**

Say each picture name. Write the letter that stands for the consonant
sound you hear in the middle of the word.

1.	2.	3.	4.
meter	ru__er	ti__er	se__en
5.	6.	7.	8.
ra__io	pi__ot	sho__el	ra__or
9.	10.	11.	12.
le__on	ro__ot	o__en	spi__er
13.	14.	15.	16.
mi__er	ba__er	pa__er	ska__er

Medial consonants **d, b, l, t, m, p, v, g, n,** and **k**

Cat begins with the hard sound of **c**. **City** begins with the soft sound of **c**. Say each picture name. Color the picture red if the name begins with the hard sound of **c**. Color the picture blue if the name begins with the soft sound of **c**.

1.	2.	3.	4.
5.	6.	7.	8.
9.	10.	11.	12.
13.	14.	15.	16.

When **c** is followed by **a, o,** or **u,** it usually has the hard sound, as in **cat.** When **c** is followed by **e, i,** or **y,** it usually has the soft sound, as in **city.** Say each picture name. Circle either **hard c** or **soft c** to show the sound of **c** in the picture name.

1. city	2. ceiling	3. vacuum	4. cot
hard c (soft c)	hard c / soft c	hard c / soft c	hard c / soft c
5. cube	6. bracelet	7. coat	8. fence
hard c / soft c	hard c / soft c	hard c / soft c	hard c / soft c
9. celery	10. car	11. rice	12. curtains
hard c / soft c	hard c / soft c	hard c / soft c	hard c / soft c
13. card	14. cymbals	15. mice	16. cat
hard c / soft c	hard c / soft c	hard c / soft c	hard c / soft c

14 Unit 2/Lesson 6

Hard and soft consonant **c**

Goat begins with the hard sound of **g**. **Gym** begins with the soft sound of **g**. Say each picture name. Color the picture red if the name begins with the hard sound of **g**. Color the picture blue if the name begins with the soft sound of **g**.

1.	2.	3.	4.
5.	6.	7.	8.
9.	10.	11.	12.
13.	14.	15.	16.

Hard and soft consonant **g**

When **g** is followed by **a, o,** or **u,** it usually has the hard sound, as in **goat.** When **g** is followed by **e, i,** or **y,** it usually has the soft sound, as in **gym.** Say each picture name. Circle either **hard g** or **soft g** to show the sound of **g** in the picture name.

1. gym	2. giant	3. wagon	4. dragon
hard g / (soft g)	hard g / soft g	hard g / soft g	hard g / soft g

5. alligator	6. gem	7. gate	8. guitar
hard g / soft g	hard g / soft g	hard g / soft g	hard g / soft g

9. engine	10. goat	11. giraffe	12. cage
hard g / soft g	hard g / soft g	hard g / soft g	hard g / soft g

13. golf	14. game	15. huge	16. goose
hard g / soft g	hard g / soft g	hard g / soft g	hard g / soft g

Read each sentence. Circle the word that completes the sentence. Then write the word on the line.

1. My _____cat_____ likes to play in the sun.   (cat) cone

2. The _____ box was too big to lift.   dance **huge**

3. My dog can _____ for its bone.   **gold** beg

4. Mike had an ice cream _____ on Wednesday.   **cone** coat

5. The car came to a stop at the red _____.   **huge** gate

6. Mary cleaned the _____ where her pet mice live.   **game** cage

7. Would you like to go to the _____ with me?   **coat** dance

8. Susan has a new _____ pin.   **golf** gold

9. Dad made _____ and meat for our meal.   **card** rice

10. Carlos wanted to open the _____ right away.   **huge** gift

11. Pam was sleeping on the small _____.   **cute** cot

12. The _____ around my home needs painting.   **fence** rice

13. Mom gave me a big _____ when she saw me.   **hug** gym

14. How long did it take you to bake the _____?   **cake** dance

Read the words in the box at the top of the page. Write each word under the correct heading.

cone	celery	gym	rice
city	cat	goat	cute
gold	giraffe	bacon	huge
engine	gate	wagon	ceiling

hard c

cat

soft c

hard g

soft g

Say each picture name. Write the missing consonant letter or letters.

1.	2.	3.	4.
__ e __	__ a __	__ i __ e __	__ ea __

5.	6.	7.	8.
__ or __ e __	__ wa __ on	__ a __ e __	__ i __

9.	10.	11.	12.
__ u __	__ ra __ io	__ o __	__ ca __ el

13.	14.	15.	16.
__ ea __	__ i __ e __	__ pi __ ot	__ o __ e __

Read each sentence. Circle the word that completes the sentence. Then
write the word on the line.

_____

1. The _____ made two stops on the way to Chicago. **bus**
   tub

2. Put your right _____ up and hop up and down. **leg**
   sit

3. Pam helped me find the little _____ on the mat. **ten**
   pin

4. My dad always puts on his _____ when he goes out. **hat**
   read

5. Look at the dog _____ for its bone. **dig**
   gate

6. I will have to get a _____ to clean up. **mop**
   mat

7. _____ is good to eat with ham. **Nap**
   Rice

8. Mom pulled a long _____ from the wall. **nail**
   lid

9. Lisa has to put some _____ in her car. **bat**
   gas

10. "Please come down from there," said my _____. **cute**
    mom

11. Dad puts a _____ on the baby when she eats. **bid**
    bib

12. Dan saw many new cars on the _____. **road**
    seat

13. My _____ likes to ride with me in the van. **huge**
    cat

14. It will _____ the two of us to carry this huge box. **take**
    beg

TEST Initial and final consonants

When vowel **a** comes between two consonants, it has the short sound of **a,** as in **cat.** Say each picture name. Circle the word that names the picture.

1.

bat (cat)
man tag

2.

hat fat
ham tan

3.

rat ran
nap van

4.

jam ham
hat mat

5.

ran tap
rat sat

6.

can pat
bag man

7.

map lap
cat mad

8.

ram rag
rat tag

9.

tab tan
rat jam

10.

can ran
tag cap

11.

sat bad
tap bat

12.

pat pan
van nap

13.

man mat
cat mad

14.

nap pan
fan fat

15.

jam rag
tap tag

16.

cab sad
cat tap

Say each picture name. Write the word that names the picture.

1. _____ cat _____	2. _____ _____	3. _____ _____	4. _____ _____
5. _____ _____	6. _____ _____	7. _____ _____	8. _____ _____
9. _____ _____	10. _____ _____	11. _____ _____	12. _____ _____
13. _____ _____	14. _____ _____	15. _____ _____	16. _____ _____

Look at the picture. Then read the sentence. Circle the word that completes the sentence. Write the word on the line.

	1. She put on her __hat__ for the show.	fan (hat) sat
	2. A _____ is on his lap.	bag map tag
	3. Can you see the fly near the _____?	can pan tan
	4. I see on the _____ where we live.	nap tap map
	5. Jen can clean the van with a _____.	rag bag can
	6. Eric spreads the _____.	ham hat jam
	7. Sam likes to sleep on the _____.	bat bag mat

Read each sentence. Circle the word that completes the sentence. Then write the word on the line.

1. Help me carry this big __bag__ .   (bag)
                                  wag
                                  rag

                                      ran
                                      pan

2. Seven of us can ride in the _____ .   van

                                      bat
                                      mat

3. My cat will sleep on the _____ .   sat

                                      man
                                      van

4. You will get a _____ if you sit in the sun.   tan

                                      ham
                                      ran

5. Dad told us not to eat all the _____ .   can

                                      cat
                                      hat

6. Pam found a tan _____ that was hurt.   pat

                                      map
                                      nap

7. After the game I took a _____ .   sap

                                      man
                                      can

8. Please buy me a drink in a _____ .   ran

                                      jam
                                      mat

9. My brother knows how to make _____ .   bat

                                      pan
                                      can

10. Please put on the _____ when it gets warm.   fan

                                      lap
                                      map

11. Will you help us read this _____ ?   tap

                                      man
                                      van

12. Dan was asked to walk, but he _____ .   ran

When vowel **e** comes between two consonants, it has the short sound of **e**, as in **hen**. Say each picture name. Circle the word that names the picture.

1.

hem   ten
(hen)   net

2.

get   wet
net   set

3.

Ben   met
hem   men

4.

red   jet
ten   pet

5.

red   bed
fed   bet

6.

led   hem
let   bed

7.

pen   den
pet   yet

8.

pat   tap
tan   tag

9.

tap   ham
can   jam

10.

ten   jet
men   set

11.

Ben   met
Meg   men

12.

pet   let
led   pen

13.

led   let
leg   beg

14.

fed   met
wet   web

15.

ten   Ben
Peg   bet

16.

beg   men
met   yet

Say each picture name. Write the word that names the picture.

1. __hen__	2.	3.	4.
5.	6.	7.	8.
9.	10.	11.	12.
13.	14.	15.	16.

Short vowel **e**

Look at the picture. Then read the sentence. Circle the word that completes the sentence. Write the word on the line.

	1. A hat will look funny on a __hen__.	(hen) pen den
	2. We cannot sing like those _____.	Ben men ten
	3. What is in the _____?	web jet wet
	4. Where do I put the first red _____?	beg leg peg
	5. It hurt its left _____ when it jumped.	bed leg peg
	6. _____ the dress if it is too long.	Hem Men Web
	7. Can a cat fly a _____?	web set jet

Read each sentence. Circle the word that completes the sentence. Then write the word on the line.

1. Look at that big red ___hen___. (hen) men met

2. Wash well before you go to _____. bed red led

3. You may hurt your _____ if you fall. beg leg peg

4. Look at that _____ fly up high. jet met bet

5. We can catch the bugs in the _____. bet net jet

6. Come take a look at the _____. web wet met

7. Bev would not _____ us see her. let set bet

8. Ken and Ted are the two _____ in the jet. hen men pen

9. A bat may not make a very good _____. get let pet

10. Four plus six make _____. Ben den ten

11. We get _____ when we wash. yet set wet

12. Do you have a _____ I could use? men pen ten

Phonics in Action

Read the story.

The Wet Pet

Wags is Len's pet.
Wags is at the red well.
Wags gets in. He is a wet mess.
He yaps and yelps for help.
Len sets a net in the well.
He gets his wet pet.
Wags is glad. He laps Len.

Write the word on the line that completes each sentence about the story.

_____

1. Wags gets in a _____ well.

_____

2. Wags _____ and yelps.

_____

3. Len gets his _____ pet.

Say the word that you make as you slide down the hill. Then circle the word. The first one shows you what to do.

1.

wig   lag   (wag)   sag

2.

wet   yet   sat   get

3.

red   let   tin   pet

4.

bat   vat   cot   cat

5.

wall   less   well   mess

6.

not   met   net   get

7.

nap   sap   lap   cap

8.

map   nap   mat   nip

REVIEW Short vowels **a** and **e**

When vowel **o** comes between two consonants, it has the short sound of **o,** as in **fox.** Say each picture name. Circle the word that names the picture.

1.
box   ox
hop   (fox)

2.
mop   fog
pop   jog

3.
jam   rag
tap   tag

4.
hot   pot
pod   top

5.
bat   ran
rat   tag

6.
job   top
jog   pot

7.
lot   mop
hog   hot

8.
ox   pot
sob   box

9.
mob   tot
box   cot

10.
fox   cob
fog   hog

11.
top   hop
mop   hot

12.
Bob   cob
Dot   hog

13.
dog   not
dot   lot

14.
pet   peg
yet   pen

15.
fox   box
lot   Bob

16.
rob   rod
mop   mob

Say each picture name. Write the word that names the picture.

1.	2.	3.	4.
fox			

5.	6.	7.	8.

9.	10.	11.	12.

13.	14.	15.	16.
	10		

Short vowel o

Look at the picture. Then read the sentence. Circle the word that completes the sentence. Write the word on the line.

	1. Six small tops are in the _box_ .	(box) fox fog
	2. Bob will take a nap on the _____ .	top cot mop
	3. Pam likes to be with her _____ .	rod mom Tom
	4. It is very _____ in the sun.	cot not hot
	5. The pig ate every last bit from the _____ .	cob job mob
	6. Small **i** has a dot at the _____ .	mop pop top
	7. It will be a big job to clean that _____ .	lot pot mop

Read each sentence. Circle the word that completes the sentence. Then write the word on the line.

1. Ken does not want to pet the ___fox___.

   box
   (fox)
   dot

2. Dad and Mom like to _____ together.

   fog
   hog
   jog

3. I will sleep on the little _____.

   cot
   hot
   lot

4. The _____ made it hard to see.

   hog
   fog
   hot

5. Put a _____ at the top of the small **j.**

   dot
   hot
   lot

6. Clean the den with a _____.

   mop
   pop
   top

7. Look at the _____ go around and around.

   hop
   top
   pop

8. Please put the ham into that _____.

   hot
   not
   pot

9. Would you like to see my pet _____?

   ox
   hot
   not

10. My cat is sleeping in its _____.

   lot
   fox
   box

11. My mom just got a new _____.

   job
   rob
   sob

12. Help me move this big _____.

   fog
   job
   log

Phonics in Action

Read the story.

Peg the Vet

Don sobs. He is sad.
Tom the cat is not well.
Don gets Tom in a box.
They go to Peg the vet.
Peg helps. She pets Tom.
She sets the bad leg.
Don is glad. Tom naps.

Write the word on the line that completes each sentence about the story.

_____

1. Tom is a _____.

_____

2. Don gets Tom in a _____.

_____

3. Peg _____ the bad leg.

Look at the picture. Then read the sentence. Circle the word that
rhymes with the underlined word. Write the word on the line.

	1. It rhymes with <u>set</u>. __vet__	vat ⟨vet⟩ peg
	2. It rhymes with <u>bat</u>. _____	cot bit cat
	3. It rhymes with <u>beg</u>. _____	leg pig pet
	4. It rhymes with <u>fox</u>. _____	box for fix
	5. It rhymes with <u>mob</u>. _____	crib rib sob
	6. It rhymes with <u>ran</u>. _____	ran can run

REVIEW Short vowels **a**, **e**, and **o**

When vowel **u** comes between two consonants, it has the short sound of **u,** as in **bug.** Say each picture name. Circle the word that names the picture.

1.	**2.**	**3.**	**4.**
rug bun but (bug)	nut hug hut but	cup rub rug tug	but bus dug bun
5.	**6.**	**7.**	**8.**
cup bun cub dug	us run nut sun	mug rug mud gum	pup gum jug up
9.	**10.**	**11.**	**12.**
ox pot sob box	cut cup but up	mud tug hum jug	tub hut rug but
13.	**14.**	**15.**	**16.**
jug hut nut hug	den hen men pen	cut cub cup nut	nut hug hut us

Say each picture name. Write the word that names the picture.

1. bug	2.	3.	4.
5.	6.	7.	8.
9.	10.	11.	12.
13.	14.	15.	16.

Short vowel u

Look at the picture. Then read the sentence. Circle the word that completes the sentence. Write the word on the line.

	1. I like to __hug__ my dad.	bug (hug) tug
	2. Bob is washing Max in the _____.	cub rub tub
	3. That box can hold the _____.	mug pup gum
	4. I sit on this _____.	dug hug rug
	5. My dog plays with the _____.	cup pup dug
	6. The van is not as big as the _____.	bus bug but
	7. The cups and the _____ are on the mat.	bug mug jug

Read each sentence. Circle the word that completes the sentence. Then write the word on the line.

1. The green __jug__ has tea in it.
bug
(jug)
tug

2. A _____ is a little dog.
but
tub
pup

3. Have a slice of ham in your _____.
bun
fun
sun

4. My cat likes to sleep on the _____.
bug
mug
rug

5. Mom rides the _____ to work every day.
bus
bug
bud

6. Ned and I have _____ playing together.
sun
fun
run

7. Please wash the _____ off the van.
bud
nut
mud

8. My hot drink is in the red _____.
hug
mug
dug

9. We get light from the _____.
fun
run
sun

10. Nan does not have any _____.
gum
jug
mug

11. The little _____ will soon grow big.
bud
but
bus

12. Little Kim sips her drink from the _____.
cut
cup
cub

Short vowel u

Phonics in Action

Read the story.

The Run

Don and Meg get set.
Don jogs. Meg runs laps.
Don jumps. Meg is on the mat.
The run is on! The pals go.
They get to the end.
They are glad they ran.

Write the word on the line that completes each sentence about the story.

_____

1. Don and Meg get set to _____.

_____

2. _____ is on the mat.

_____

3. The pals are _____ they ran.

Say the word that you make as you slide down the hill. Then circle the word. The first one shows you what to do.

1.

sap   rap   lip   (lap)

2.

cat   mitt   mat   cot

3.

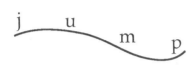

jump   bump   jam   limp

4.

set   get   vet   sat

5.

job   bog   jig   jog

6.

glib   crab   grab   glad

7.

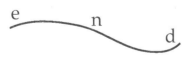

and   send   end   sand

8.

fun   run   ran   ton

Short vowels **a**, **e**, **o**, and **u**

When vowel **i** comes between two consonants, it has the short sound of **i,** as in **pig.** Say each picture name. Circle the word that names the picture.

1.	2.	3.	4.
wig (pig) pit pin	bit lip bib fib	sit tin him hit	rim rip pit pig
5.	6.	7.	8.
did lit hip lid	but bus gum dug	lid lips sip pin	pin nip pit pig
9.	10.	11.	12.
rib did bib rip	fix six sip sit	bib pit rip rib	mop fog hop fox
13.	14.	15.	16.
pig dig dim dip	nip tin fit fin	pin sit him pit	wig pig win sip

Say each picture name. Write the word that names the picture.

1. _____ pig	**2.** _____ _____	**3.** _____ _____	**4.** _____ _____
5. _____ _____	**6.** _____ _____	**7.** _____ _____	**8.** _____ _____
9. _____ _____	**10.** _____ _____	**11.** _____ _____	**12.** _____ _____
13. _____ _____	**14.** _____ _____	**15.** _____ _____	**16.** _____ _____

Short vowel **i**

Look at the picture. Then read the sentence. Circle the word that completes the sentence. Write the word on the line.

	1. Look in the pen and you will see a __pig__ .	(pig) wig dig
	2. Please put the _____ on the pot.	bid bib lid
	3. I can fix your leg with my _____ .	bit rib kit
	4. Can you see where I _____ the box?	hid lid rid
	5. What will the pups find when they _____?	sip jig dig
	6. Don't fall in the _____ .	bit pin pit
	7. Tim will look funny in the _____ .	wig pig win

Read each sentence. Circle the word that completes the sentence. Then write the word on the line.

1. Three plus three make ___**six**___.
    sip
    sit
    (six)

2. My new rug has a big _____.
    rim
    rip
    rib

3. I like Jim and I want to play with _____.
    him
    hip
    hit

4. You could hurt a _____ if you fall from up there.
    bib
    rib
    fit

5. I just want to _____ after the long walk.
    sit
    bit
    lit

6. Dad cannot find the _____ for the pan.
    bid
    hid
    lid

7. The light is _____ but I can still see.
    did
    dig
    dim

8. Mom looks pretty in her new _____.
    jig
    pig
    wig

9. I could not find my dog when it _____.
    hip
    hid
    him

10. Have Tim put on a _____ to keep clean.
    bib
    bin
    bit

11. Just take a _____ if you don't want a lot to drink.
    dip
    lip
    sip

12. Is your new hat too big or does it _____?
    fit
    hit
    lit

Say each picture name. Write the missing vowel to complete the word that names each picture.

1.	2.	3.	4.
hut	v_n	n_t	b_x

5.	6.	7.	8.
b_b	h_t	s_n	p_n

9.	10.	11.	12.
m_t	p_n	f_x	b_n

13.	14.	15.	16.
t_n	h_m	l_g	s_x

Change the vowel in each word to make a new word. Write the new word on the line.

1. tab **tub**

2. pet _____

3. hut _____

4. bid _____

5. cob _____

6. pin _____

7. jug _____

8. pot _____

9. map _____

10. cup _____

11. top _____

12. hem _____

13. set _____

14. bat _____

15. cot _____

16. fin _____

17. lip _____

18. bug _____

19. nut _____

20. men _____

21. dad _____

22. fat _____

23. led _____

24. rod _____

25. pug _____

26. ton _____

REVIEW Short vowels **a, e, o, u,** and **i**

Phonics in Action

Read the story.

Ron at Bat

Pat and Ron are pals.
They go to the mud lot.
Pat has a tan bat.
Ron has a mitt and hat.
Ron tells Pat to bat.
A miss! Ron will bat.
Ron gets a hit! He runs.
The pals yell. It is fun.

Write the word on the line that completes each sentence about the story.

_____

1. Ron has a _____ and hat.

_____

2. Ron _____ Pat to bat.

_____

3. The pals yell and have _____.

Look at the picture. Then read the sentence. Circle the word that rhymes with the underlined word. Then write the word on the line.

	1. It rhymes with <u>cat</u>. bat	(bat) bit sit
	2. It rhymes with <u>sit</u>.	get mitt sat
	3. It rhymes with <u>fun</u>.	fan ran run
	4. It rhymes with <u>lot</u>.	cat cot lit
	5. It rhymes with <u>tell</u>.	tall till yell
	6. It rhymes with <u>fin</u>.	pan pin fun

REVIEW Short vowels **a, e, o, u,** and **i**

Say each picture name. Write the word that names the picture.

1. _____ _____	2. _____ _____	3. _____ _____	4. _____ _____
5. _____ _____	6. _____ _____	7. _____ _____	8. _____ _____
9. _____ _____	10. _____ _____	11. _____ _____	12. _____ _____
13. _____ _____	14. _____ _____	15. _____ _____	16. _____ _____

Read each sentence. Find a word in the box that completes it. Write
the word on the line.

run	bit	hen	cot	has	bed
hat	bus	wet	him	rug	dot

1. A _____ is not as big as a bed.

2. Please do not walk on the new _____.

3. A _____ may not make a very good pet.

4. You can ride in the _____ or in the van.

5. Tom ran so fast that I could not catch _____.

6. The blanket will be too heavy to pick up the if it is _____.

7. Carol put on her _____ when it got cold.

8. After Beth _____ her lip, it got red.

9. A bug can be as small as a _____.

10. Take the spread off the _____ before you go to sleep.

11. The little pig wants what the big pig _____.

12. My dog will _____ after a cat.

TEST Short vowels **a**, **e**, **o**, **u**, and **i**

When a word has two vowels, the first vowel often has the long sound and the second is silent, as in **hay, rain,** and **cage.** Say each picture name. Circle the word that names the picture.

1.	2.	3.	4.
(hay) say	rat mat	pan ran	page rage
ham Sam	mail rail	pay ray	pan ran

5.	6.	7.	8.
date gate	save cave	fate bait	rain bag
dab gab	cap sap	bat fat	bait rag

9.	10.	11.	12.
day hail	sat same	ran rain	jay hay
clam ham	vase van	main man	jam ham

13.	14.	15.	16.
pail tail	mat bat	can cap	tap mail
pan tan	bay may	cane cape	map sail

NAME _____

Say each picture name. Circle the letter or letters that stand for the vowel sound. Then write the letter or letters on the line to complete the word.

1. a **(ay)**	2. a ay	3. a ai	4. a a-e
b a y	f __ n	n __ l	l __ k

5. a ai	6. a ay	7. a a-e	8. a ai
s __ l	p __	c __ n	m __ p

9. a ay	10. a a-e	11. a ai	12. a a-e
c __ t	g __ m	r __ l	c __ g

13. a ay	14. a a-e	15. a ai	16. a a-e
w __	b __ g	t __ l	c __ p

Long vowel **a**

Look at the picture. Then read the sentence. Circle the word that
completes the sentence. Write the word on the line.

1. Look at the bat on the __gate__.		pail (gate) cage
2. Please _____ if you want to ride on the bus.		pay say gave
3. If it starts to _____, go in the cave.		sail fail hail
4. Can you find a _____?		lace race vase
5. Lee hurt her leg and must walk with a _____.		cane lane rail
6. Where is the _____ on this map?		lake mail rake
7. I will bake a cake after I read this _____.		cage page bait

Read each sentence. Circle the word that completes the sentence. Then write the word on the line.

1. Pat jumped into the ___lake___. bake (lake) take

2. I wish I could fly like a blue _____. jay ray day

3. Please take the _____ to Ms. Howard. fail mail tail

4. The cat is warm under my _____. cave cane cape

5. Did you eat the pie we _____? fade made paid

6. I have the _____ pail that you have. same fame game

7. If you want to laugh, look at the _____. ape ate late

8. It is going to _____ so we cannot play. sail rain rail

9. Dan will save some _____ for you. wake cake take

10. The yellow van will be going this _____. say ray way

11. Will Dave _____ on the bay or the lake? sail rail bail

12. We can make a date one day in _____. hay ray May

When a word has two vowels, the first vowel often has the long sound and the second is silent, as in **bee** and **beak.** Say each picture name. Circle the word that names the picture.

1.	2.	3.	4.
Ben den (bee) deep	set neat seat net	men let mean lean	met set beat meat
5.	6.	7.	8.
sea set pea pet	bead read bed red	let bee see set	seat beet met set
9.	10.	11.	12.
let peek pet leak	wed bed bead weed	team heap hen ten	led red reef leaf
13.	14.	15.	16.
ten seal Ben bee	led bean lean bed	hem heel peel pen	leg beg lean bean

Say each picture name. Circle the letter or letters that stand for the vowel sound. Then write the letter or letters on the line to complete the word.

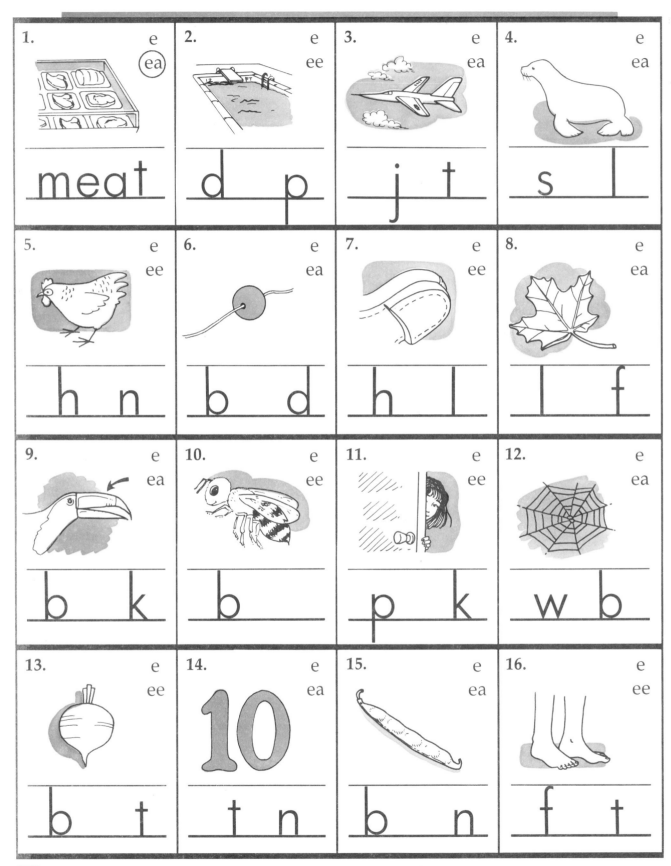

1. e (ea) meat

2. e ee d _ p

3. e ea j _ t

4. e ea s _ l

5. e ee h _ n

6. e ea b _ d

7. e ee h _ l

8. e ea l _ f

9. e ea b _ k

10. e ee b _

11. e ee p _ k

12. e ea w _ b

13. e ee b _ t

14. e ea t _ n

15. e ea b _ n

16. e ee f _ t

Look at the picture. Then read the sentence. Circle the word that completes the sentence. Write the word on the line.

	1. I do not like this _heat_.	(heat) beef lean
	2. Kate will walk on the _____.	team beam lean
	3. This is your _____, not that one.	seat beat meat
	4. Look out for that big _____!	bean beak peek
	5. We like to play hide and _____.	peek seek need
	6. What will grow from that small _____?	beat meat seed
	7. Dad drinks _____ from a cup.	peas tea sea

Read each sentence. Circle the word that completes the sentence. Then write the word on the line.

1. Can you see the yellow and black ___**bee**___ ?
    fee
    see
    (bee)

2. I will keep the pretty _____ .
    leaf
    reef
    deal

3. Put your hot _____ in the cold lake.
    feet
    beat
    heat

4. When Jean grows up, she wants to sail on the _____ .
    tea
    sea
    pea

5. Bob likes to _____ before he goes to sleep.
    read
    lead
    bead

6. Will you please take your _____ ?
    beat
    seat
    heat

7. I always eat a good _____ .
    meal
    seal
    real

8. Karen cannot wait to see the new _____ play.
    seam
    beam
    team

9. Ham and beef are both _____ .
    beat
    seat
    meat

10. Look at the big yellow _____ on that bird.
    beak
    peek
    leak

11. Do not go where the sea is _____ .
    heap
    deep
    sleep

12. When Kate and I raced, she _____ me.
    beat
    seat
    heat

Phonics in Action

Read the story.

The Feast

The sky is rainy and gray.
Dee and Jake need a feast.
Jake makes meat and gravy.
Dee makes greens and leeks.
They bake a sweet cake.
They get grapes and dates.
The pals eat a late meal.
The day seems less gray.

Write the word on the line that completes each sentence about the story.

_____

1. Jake and Dee _____ a feast.

_____

2. The pals _____ a sweet cake.

_____

3. They _____ grapes and dates.

Look at the picture. Find the number and follow the arrow. Write the word on the puzzle.

Across

2. →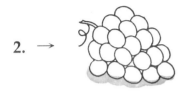

3. →

4. →

Down

1. ↓

2. ↓

REVIEW Long vowels **a**, **e**, **o**, **u**, and **i**

When a word has two vowels, the first vowel often has the long sound and the second is silent, as in **goat** and **rose.** Say each picture name. Circle the word that names the picture.

1.	2.	3.	4.
joke jog (goat) load	hot home dome dot	moan tone mop top	nose not rose rot
5.	6.	7.	8.
hope rod hop rope	rope sob soap rob	box fox bone cone	coal pole cot pot
9.	10.	11.	12.
Bob cob coat boat	hose pose hop pop	bone loaf lob Bob	hole hot pot pole
13.	14.	15.	16.
sob soak poke pod	code cob rode rod	not cot note coat	toad road Tod rod

Say each picture name. Circle the letter or letters that stand for the vowel sound. Then write the letter or letters on the line to complete the word.

1. o (oa)
goat

2. o o-e
n _ _ t

3. o oa
s _ _ k

4. o o-e
d _ _ t

5. o o-e
n _ _ s

6. o oa
b _ _ x

7. o oa
s _ _ p

8. o o-e
d _ _ m

9. o o-e
h _ _ l

10. o oa
l _ _ f

11. o o-e
p _ _ t

12. o oa
t _ _ d

13. o oa
s _ _ ck

14. o oa
c _ _ t

15. o o-e
r _ _ s

16. o o-e
y _ _ k

Look at the picture. Then read the sentence. Circle the word that completes the sentence. Write the word on the line.

1. My dog dug a deep **hole**.		role (hole) pole
2. Please help me carry this big _____.		road load loaf
3. Did you ever see a toad jump _____?		cone rope dome
4. After the game, can you come _____ with me?		home dome bone
5. We looked in the mail for a _____ from Pam.		poke goat note
6. Did you eat most of this _____?		loan load loaf
7. Soak the _____ to clean it.		vote goat coat

Read each sentence. Circle the word that completes the sentence. Then write the word on the line.

1. Jay wants the ___ role ___ of Father in the play.   sole (role) dole

2. We have a date to ride in your new _____.   coat moat boat

3. Tim was cold so he put on a _____.   rope robe hope

4. I _____ you will like my pretty cape.   hope soap cope

5. My dog has a cold, black _____.   rope rose nose

6. Sam will _____ me his brown hat.   cone loan bone

7. My mom said she will _____ for you.   note boat vote

8. Wash the dog all over with _____.   hope rope soap

9. Jake will get a big _____ for his pet.   loan bone dome

10. It is cold out here so I will go _____.   dome home roam

11. We will _____ this cart with hay.   nose road load

12. There is a lot of black _____ in the cave.   goal coal goat

Phonics in Action

Read the story.

Planting Seeds

Joan and Jay poke a hole for each seed.
They take out the weeds.
The rays send the heat.
Jay hopes for rain, but Joan tips a pail to soak the seeds.
They see a green leaf!
They reap beets, peas, and beans.

Write the word on the line that completes each sentence about the story.

_____

1. Joan and Jay _____ holes.

_____

2. Jay hopes for _____.

_____

3. They see a green _____.

Look at the picture. Then read the sentence. Circle the word that
rhymes with the underlined word. Write the word on the line.

1. It rhymes with <u>hope</u>. _____ soap _____

soak
(soap)
top

2. It rhymes with <u>sees</u>. _____

pens
sets
peas

3. It rhymes with <u>rain</u>. _____

read
cane
cone

4. It rhymes with <u>beet</u>. _____

feet
bait
boat

5. It rhymes with <u>make</u>. _____

rock
rake
joke

6. It rhymes with <u>bone</u>. _____

home
cone
bean

REVIEW Long vowels **a**, **e**, and **o**

When a word has two vowels, the first vowel often has the long sound and the second is silent, as in **mule.** Say each picture name. Circle the word that names the picture.

1.	2.	3.	4.
rug mug (mule) rule	tune huge tug hug	page pat cube cub	rub tub rude tube
5.	6.	7.	8.
dune dug tune tug	beg leg bean leaf	goat loaf got lot	fun hut fuse cute
9.	10.	11.	12.
nut cube cute cut	bee nut sea dune	tune cub cup cube	gate tub gas tube
13.	14.	15.	16.
beak rude bet rub	cute rain ran bus	lug rob hug robe	bug note fuse not

Say each picture name. Circle the letter or letters that stand for the vowel sound. Then write the letter or letters on the line to complete the word.

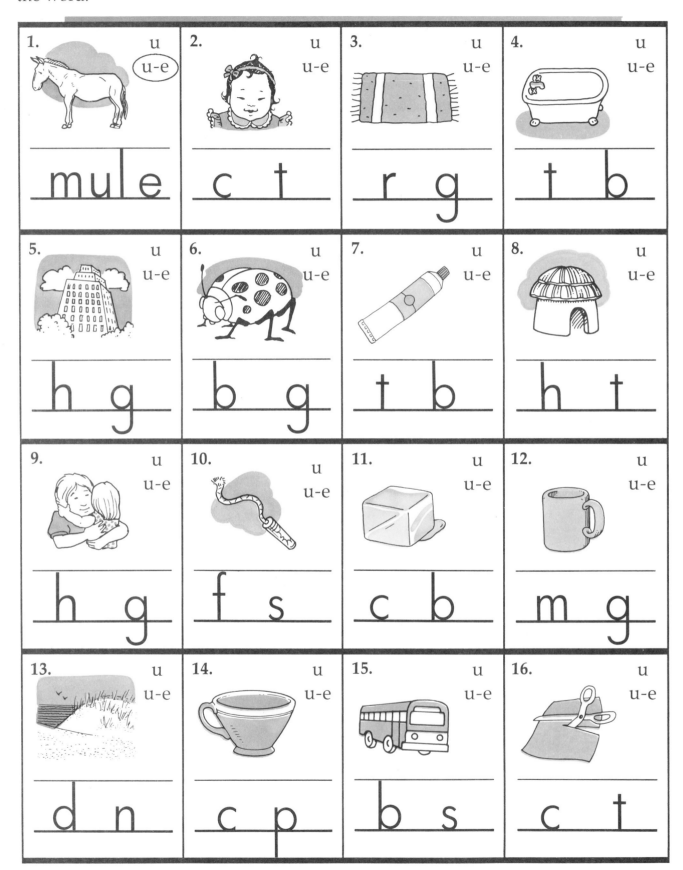

1. u (u-e)   mule

2. u u-e   c___t

3. u u-e   r___g

4. u u-e   t___b

5. u u-e   h___g

6. u u-e   b___g

7. u u-e   t___b

8. u u-e   h___t

9. u u-e   h___g

10. u u-e   f___s

11. u u-e   c___b

12. u u-e   m___g

13. u u-e   d___n

14. u u-e   c___p

15. u u-e   b___s

16. u u-e   c___t

Look at the picture. Then read the sentence. Circle the word that completes the sentence. Write the word on the line.

	1. Will you please give me the ___cube___ ?	cub dune (cube)
	2. I want to eat this _____ bun.	huge hug rug
	3. Bob will get the _____ back on the road.	rule mule tune
	4. José made a new _____ for our game.	rug rule cute
	5. Pam has a _____ pet toad.	cube cut cute
	6. There is not too much in the _____ .	tub tube tune
	7. We like to hum a funny _____ .	mule tune fuse

Read each sentence. Circle the word that completes the sentence. Then write the word on the line.

1. It is fun to run on the ___dune___.
   dug
   tune
   (dune)

2. Joe can sleep on the cot in the _____.
   hum
   hut
   huge

3. That _____ little cat has green eyes.
   cut
   cute
   cube

4. The train set came in a _____ box.
   huge
   hug
   hum

5. Our team had to learn a new _____.
   dug
   dune
   rule

6. Will you _____ the cake for us?
   cute
   cut
   cub

7. If your feet hurt, _____ them.
   rub
   tub
   tube

8. Kay is feeding some hay to the _____.
   fuse
   mule
   tube

9. Jay cannot open the green _____.
   tune
   tube
   huge

10. Rosa likes to pet the tame _____ at the zoo.
    cub
    cube
    rule

11. Do you know the name of that _____?
    hug
    tug
    tune

12. The woman carefully replaced the _____.
    fuse
    cute
    tug

Long vowel **u**

Phonics in Action

Read the story.

Dune Maze

Jude and Bea lead a team.
They go past the dunes.
Jude peeks in a cave.
The cave is a maze.
They roam all day.
The team is in a daze.
Jude hums a tune.
Bea shows the way.

Write the word on the line that completes each sentence about the story.

1. Jude and Bea _____ a team.

2. They go past the _____ .

3. The cave is a _____ .

Look at the picture. Then read the clue for each number. Write the rhyming word in the puzzle.

Across

2. →  rhymes with *brave*

4. →  rhymes with *tune*

5. →  rhymes with *bead*

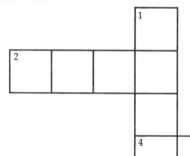

Down

1. ↓  rhymes with *lead*

3. ↓ 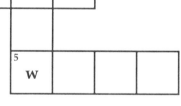 rhymes with *show*

When a word has two vowels, the first vowel often has the long sound and the second is silent, as in **kite.** Say each picture name. Circle the word that names the picture.

1.

(mice)   rip
rice   dip

2.

lit   like
bike   bib

3.

lip   nine
fine   nip

4.

kite   pit
kit   pipe

5.

lid   fine
fin   line

6.

bite   kite
bit   kit

7.

hive   live
lip   hip

8.

nice   rice
nip   rip

9.

tin   pin
tire   pine

10.

five   fit
pine   pit

11.

tip   mine
him   vine

12.

fin   tin
tile   file

13.

fig   wig
five   wire

14.

dim   lime
dime   lip

15.

tire   fire
fin   tin

16.

dive   lip
dip   live

Say each picture name. Circle the letter or letters that stand for the vowel sound. Then write the letter or letters on the line to complete the word.

1. i (i-e) dime	**2.** i i-e f v	**3.** i i-e s t	**4.** i i-e t r
5. i i-e b b	**6.** i i-e h v	**7.** i i-e b k	**8.** i i-e v n
9. i i-e p p	**10.** i i-e m c	**11.** i i-e l n	**12.** i i-e f n
13. i i-e k t	**14.** i i-e n n	**15.** i i-e f r	**16.** i i-e l d

Long vowel i

Look at the picture. Then read the sentence. Circle the word that completes the sentence. Write the word on the line.

1. The big dog will not ___bite___ you.		(bite) kite vice
2. I need a _____ to pay the man.		lime pine dime
3. Do not go on the _____ without a rope.		hike like bike
4. I want to pick just one green _____.		time lime dime
5. I have a _____ toad in my hand.		five hive live
6. Carla Ramaz will put out the _____.		fire tire wire
7. Can you walk on the _____?		mine line mile

Long vowel i   Unit 4/Lesson 27   **77**

Read each sentence. Circle the word that completes the sentence. Then write the word on the line.

1. Do you have ___**time**___ to play with the cube?
   dime
   (time)
   lime

2. We will fly the _____ on a windy day.
   kite
   bite
   pipe

3. Dad can _____ down very deep.
   five
   live
   dive

4. It was _____ of Julie to let us use her game.
   nice
   vine
   line

5. The old mule will eat that big _____ of hay.
   file
   time
   pile

6. Little _____ ran all over the cage.
   nice
   mice
   rice

7. Would you _____ hot tea with your meal?
   like
   hike
   bike

8. Mom will _____ Kay to do the work.
   time
   fire
   hire

9. Our van needs a new _____.
   hire
   tire
   fire

10. Three plus two make _____.
   dive
   five
   live

11. A _____ is the same as ten cents.
   dine
   dime
   dive

12. Fay can ride all the way home on her _____.
   like
   Mike
   bike

Long vowel **i**

Phonics in Action

Read the story.

The Space Ride

Noel and Judy read.
They ride deep into space.
The ship blows a fuse.
It lands in a nice place.
Noel makes a fire.
Judy hikes for miles.
They dine with space mice.
They all have a fine time.

Write the word on the line that completes each sentence about the story.

_____

1. Noel and Judy _____ into space.

_____

2. The ship _____ a fuse.

_____

3. Noel _____ a fire.

Look at the picture. Then read the sentence. Circle the word that
rhymes with the underlined word. Then write the word on the line.

1. It rhymes with lead. __read__

raid
(read)
load

2. It rhymes with tire. _____

fine
fire
wore

3. It rhymes with rice. _____

mice
mite
race

4. It rhymes with place. _____

plane
vise
vase

5. It rhymes with use. _____

fuse
food
tune

6. It rhymes with make. _____

mine
cake
like

Say the name of the picture in each box. Circle the pictures with names that have the same sound of **y.**

Y as long vowel **e** or **i**

When **y** is at the end of a word, it can stand for the long sound of **i**, as in **dry**, or the long sound of **e**, as in **pony**. Say each picture name. Circle **long e** or **long i** to show the sound of **y** in each picture name.

1.	2.	3.	4.
long e (long i)	long e long i	long e long i	long e long i

5.	6.	7.	8.
long e long i	long e long i	long e long i	long e long i

9.	10.	11.	12.
long e long i	long e long i	long e long i	long e long i

13.	14.	15.	16.
long e long i	long e long i	long e long i	long e long i

Y as long vowel **e** or **i**

Say each picture name. Circle the word that names the picture.

1. happy (jelly) silly	**2.** fry sky dry	**3.** bunny funny sunny	**4.** pry shy fly
5. by my why	**6.** hockey army monkey	**7.** fairy hairy dairy	**8.** dry sly fly
9. bunny donkey pony	**10.** dry fry why	**11.** pry sky by	**12.** hockey bunny turkey
13. dry pry shy	**14.** baby army pony	**15.** bunny funny penny	**16.** cry fly dry

Read each sentence. Circle the word that completes the sentence. Then write the word on the line.

1. A baby dog is called a ___puppy___. guppy (puppy)

2. We will take a hike on the first _____ day. sunny bunny

3. I always laugh when a joke is _____. funny penny

4. Will Sid see many trees in the _____? city fairy

5. My mom gave me a little white _____. sunny bunny

6. The jet will fly up in the _____. sky dry

7. My dad gave me a very old _____ to save. penny bunny

8. The baby fell, but she did not _____. dry cry

9. Ten plus ten make _____. pony twenty

10. Jane played the _____ in the play. fairy city

11. Put the wet coat out in the sun to _____. dry fly

12. My sister and I like to ride the _____. pony honey

13. Dad will _____ the meat in a pan. sky fry

14. Will you please put the bib on the _____? army baby

Y as long vowel **e** or **i**

The vowel letters **ei** can stand for the long sound of **a,** as in **vein,** or the long sound of **e,** as in **ceiling.** Say each picture name. Circle **long a** or **long e** to show the sound of **ei** in each picture name.

1. vein	2. sleigh	3. ceiling	4. eight
(long a) long e	long a long e	long a long e	long a long e
5. weigh	6. receipt	7. freight	8. reindeer
long a long e	long a long e	long a long e	long a long e

Read each sentence. Choose one of the **ei** words above to complete the sentence. Write the **ei** word on the line.

1. After you buy the ham, bring the ___receipt___ to Mom.

2. Does a fox _____ as much as a bear?

3. Can you find a blue _____ on your leg?

4. Can you see the bee on the _____?

5. Two plus six make _____.

6. We like to feed the _____ at the zoo.

The vowel letters **ie** can stand for the long sound of **e,** as in **niece,** or the long sound of **i,** as in **pie.** Say each picture name. Circle **long e** or **long i** to show the sound of **ie** in each picture name.

1. niece	2. pie	3. collie	4. field	5. necktie
(long e) long i	long e long i	long e long i	long e long i	long e long i

6. tie	7. chief	8. lie	9. pliers	10. piece
long e long i	long e long i	long e long i	long e long i	long e long i

Read each sentence. Choose one of the **ie** words above to complete the sentence. Write the **ie** word on the line.

1. The fire was put out by the _____ chief _____.

2. Little Tommy looked older in his new _____.

3. Mom could fix the pipes if she had _____.

4. Bobby and Jan helped bake the _____.

5. Do you know what grows in this _____?

6. Luis wants a dog called a _____ .

The vowel letters **ea** can stand for the long sound of **a,** as in **steak,** the long sound of **e,** as in **leaf,** or the short sound of **e,** as in **spread.** Say each picture name. Circle **long a, long e,** or **short e** to show the sound of **ea** in each picture name.

1. long a (long e) short e	2. long a long e short e	3. long a long e short e	4. long a long e short e	5. long a long e short e
beads	steak	bread	bedspread	beak
6. long a long e short e	7. long a long e short e	8. long a long e short e	9. long a long e short e	10. long a long e short e
daybreak	breakfast	steam	break	sweater

Read each sentence. Choose one of the **ea** words above to complete the sentence. Write the **ea** word on the line.

1. The sun comes up at daybreak.

2. Eggs, toast, and tea make a good _____.

3. Ted ate all his green beans and _____.

4. You can tell tea is too hot to drink if you can see _____.

5. The _____ is too big for the cot.

6. If the cup falls, it will _____.

Read the three words in each box. Circle all three words if they rhyme.

1. (chief leaf reef)	**2.** lie pie tie	**3.** receipt sleigh weigh	**4.** pie cry lie
5. sheik eight vein	**6.** feather leather weather	**7.** beak leak sheik	**8.** eight freight weight
9. break lake steak	**10.** neigh sleigh weigh	**11.** date late great	**12.** die lie chief
13. field shield yield	**14.** beat neat great	**15.** great freight eight	**16.** bed bread lead

Say each picture name. Circle the letters that stand for the vowel sound. Then write the letters on the line to complete the word.

1. ai ee	2. o-e ay	3. ai ie	4. u-e oa
h __ l	b __ n	f __ d	m __ l

5. i-e ea	6. ea o-e	7. u-e ai	8. ie ea
b __ k	l __ f	r __ n	st __ m

9. ei ea	10. oa ie	11. ea ay	12. a-e ie
s __ t	p __	st __ k	g __ t

13. ie ay	14. ie oa	15. oa ei	16. oa ei
r __	c o ll	c __ t	v __ n

Read each sentence. Circle the word that completes the sentence. Then write the word on the line.

1. Dee will let you ride her new _____.   **like**
                                                        bike

2. How much does the baby goat _____?   **sleigh**
                                                       weigh

3. Mike can hum a pretty _____.   **dune**
                                               tune

4. The _____ is very warm in July and August.   **weather**
                                                              feather

5. I want to see the little blue _____ fly.   **say**
                                                           jay

6. Please put some _____ on the bun.   **jelly**
                                                     penny

7. Mrs. Drake says it is not right to tell a _____.   **tie**
                                                                    lie

8. Do not pull a cat by its _____.   **tail**
                                                   pail

9. My niece is the first one on the _____.   **team**
                                                           seam

10. Some people use _____ to heat their homes.   **coal**
                                                               goal

11. Can Tom eat that great big _____?   **break**
                                                      steak

12. I know you can do it if you _____.   **try**
                                                       sky

13. Will you _____ for me next week?   **goat**
                                                     vote

14. Do you want a big or small _____ of pie?   **piece**
                                                             niece

TEST Long vowels **a, e, o, u, i,** and **y**

Say each picture name. Write the letters that stand for the beginning consonant blend.

1.	2.	3.	4.
dr	___	___	___
___	___	___	___

5.	6.	7.	8.
___	___	___	___
___	___	___	___

9.	10.	11.	12.
___	___	___	___
___	___	___	___

13.	14.	15.	16.
___	___	___	___
___	___	___	___

Initial consonant blends **fr**, **br**, **gr**, **cr**, **dr**, **pr**, and **tr**

Say each picture name. Circle the word that names the picture.

1. (train)   drop
   crane   drip

2. prize   crib
   grab   frame

3. drip   train
   cry   prize

4. drum   frog
   prize   grass

5. dry   pray
   bride   truck

6. frog   drip
   pretzel groom

7. fry   drain
   braid   tree

8. grapes   crib
   frame   brick

Read each sentence. Choose a word you circled to complete each sentence. Write the word on the line.

1. Rita wanted to win the ____ prize ____.

2. Dad saw a pine _____ at the top of the hill.

3. I will eat some _____ after my meal.

4. The baby is sleeping in his _____.

5. Dad asked me not to play the _____ before breakfast.

6. Rosa will be the _____ at the wedding on Sunday.

Initial consonant blends fr, br, gr, cr, dr, pr, and tr

Say each picture name. Write the letters that stand for the beginning consonant blend.

1. s|	2. ___	3. ___	4. ___
5. ___	6. ___	7. ___	8. ___
9. ___	10. ___	11. ___	12. ___
13. ___	14. ___	15. ___	16. ___

Initial consonant blends **fl**, **pl**, **sl**, **cl**, **bl**, and **gl**

Say each picture name. Circle the word that names the picture.

1. (clip) plug sleep glove	**2.** plus globe slip blade	**3.** plus glove clash fly	**4.** clay slam plug blade
5. flag slip play clap	**6.** blade glad float slide	**7.** sled clap plop flash	**8.** flag clock plate globe

Read each sentence. Choose a word you circled to complete each sentence. Write the word on the line.

1. We found the United States on the  globe .

2. Lisa broke the red _____ today.

3. José likes to _____ his boat in the water.

4. Use a _____ to hold these tags together.

5. Two _____ two make four.

6. Who would like to pull the _____ for Jim?

Say each picture name. Write the letters that stand for the beginning consonant blend.

1. _____
st

2. _____

3. _____

4. _____

5. _____

6. _____

7. _____

8. _____

9. _____

10. _____

11. _____

12. _____

13. _____

14. _____

15. _____

16. _____

Say each picture name. Circle the word that names the picture.

1. smile (snap) spin queen	**2.** sweep speak stove sneak	**3.** spy steam swan spin	**4.** steam snail queen skate
5. sweet snail spoke sweep	**6.** scare queen smoke stove	**7.** swim queen skin smile	**8.** spoke snake skate swan

Read each sentence. Choose a word you circled to complete each sentence. Write the word on the line.

1. Do you know how to ___ skate ___ on the ice?

2. Dad used our new _____ to heat the meat.

3. Jill will help Robert _____ the steps.

4. The rope will _____ if you pull too hard.

5. Look at Bill _____ around on the dance floor.

6. A _____ does not have any legs on which to walk.

Say each picture name. Circle the letters that stand for the beginning consonant blend. Then write the letters on the line.

1. _____ thr (str) spl str	**2.** _____ thr str shr	**3.** _____ spr thr squ	**4.** _____ squ spl thr
5. _____ scr spl _____ str	**6.** _____ thr str _____ shr	**7.** _____ scr spl _____ str	**8.** _____ spl str _____ spr
9. _____ thr spl _____ spr	**10.** _____ shr str _____ scr	**11.** _____ str spl _____ scr	**12.** _____ shr scr _____ thr
13. _____ thr scr _____ shr	**14.** _____ thr str _____ scr	**15.** _____ shr squ _____ scr	**16.** _____ str thr _____ scr

Read each sentence. Circle the word that completes the sentence. Then write the word on the line.

1. Jane and Tina like to take long walks in the ___spring___ .

throw
(spring)

2. There are many houses on my _____ .

street
sprint

3. A _____ has four sides.

square
squid

4. Ted will _____ the tub after his shower.

spring
scrub

5. "Please don't _____ me," said Lisa to her cat.

scratch
stretch

6. The _____ with all the gems is for the queen.

thread
throne

7. My new coat will not _____ when I wash it.

shrink
string

8. You must _____ all the water out of the mop.

square
squeeze

9. Bill let out a _____ when he saw the huge ape.

string
scream

10. Mrs. White _____ the log with her ax.

split
spray

11. "Quick, _____ the ball to me," said Dan.

straw
throw

12. Do you want to be _____ when you grow up?

strong
spot

13. My dog likes to _____ in its tub.

square
splash

14. Would you like to have some _____ for lunch today?

shrimp
throne

Initial consonant blends **squ, spr, str, spl, scr, shr,** and **thr**

Say each picture name. Circle the letters that stand for the ending consonant blend. Then write the letters on the line.

1.

st
(nk)
lf

nk ____

2.

nd ____
ld ____
st ____

3.

ng ____
mp ____
lk ____

4.

lk ____
st ____
lf ____

5.

nd ____
nk ____
ng ____

6.

nt ____
st ____
sk ____

7.

nt ____
ng ____
nd ____

8.

ld ____
lf ____
lk ____

9.

nt ____
nd ____
ng ____

10.

ng ____
nd ____
nt ____

11.

lk ____
ld ____
lf ____

12.

st ____
lf ____
sk ____

13.

lf ____
lk ____
ng ____

14.

nd ____
nk ____
mp ____

15.

lk ____
lf ____
ld ____

16.

lk ____
ld ____
nk ____

Final consonant blends **lf, mp, nt, st, nk, lk, sk, nd, ld,** and **ng**

Read each sentence. Circle the word that completes the sentence. Then
write the word on the line.

1. The _____king_____ and queen are going on a trip.　(king)　wing

2. We found five eggs in the little _____.　frost　nest

3. I need three cups of _____ to make this cake.　milk　silk

4. Can you get me a _____ when you go out?　stamp　stump

5. Hold up your _____ when you want to stop.　pond　hand

6. This _____ needs a lot of light.　slant　plant

7. The _____ laughed and said, "Come with me."　elf　shelf

8. Mrs. Long _____ Liz that she was a good helper.　told　hold

9. We like to _____ together once a week.　sting　sing

10. Linda sat down at her _____ and started to work.　mask　desk

11. Dad gave me a pretty dress made of _____.　silk　milk

12. Do you know how to _____ rope?　bump　jump

13. Bob found a _____ pin on the road.　gold　sold

14. Will you carry that big _____ to my home?　shrunk　trunk

Phonics in Action

Read the story.

Fun with a Friend

Fran and Hank skate.
They play in the park.
Hank can climb to the sky.
Fran can pump on a swing.
The best is a train.
The friends hang on.
They slide to the ground.
Fran and Hank share the fun.

Write the word on the line that completes each sentence about the story.

1. Fran and Hank play in the _____.

2. Fran can _____ on a swing.

3. The friends _____ to the ground.

Say the word that you make as you slide down the hill. Then circle
the word. The first one shows you what to do.

1.  (best) nest neat desk	**2.**  Hank honk hang long
3.  swing sling swung king	**4.**  snap sled slide slid
5.  bland pane plan clan	**6.** 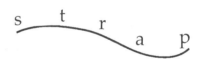 stripe scrap strap slap
7. 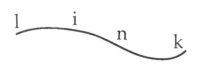 leak lick slick link	**8.**  hand sand Fran hind

REVIEW Initial and final consonant blends

Say each picture name. Write the letters that stand for the missing
beginning or ending consonant blend.

1. _____ arf	2. wi _____	3. pla _____	4. _____ ide
5. ne _____	6. stu _____	7. _____ ing	8. _____ oke
9. _____ ag	10. _____ co	11. sa _____	12. _____ ead
13. de _____	14. _____ ay	15. _____ in	16. _____ mi

Unit 5/Lesson 38 **103**

Read each sentence. Circle the word that completes the sentence. Then write the word on the line.

_____

1. Do you know how to _____ this song? **wing**
   sing

2. Put a _____ around your neck when you go out. **skin**
   scarf

3. After a long hike, Rosa put her feet in the _____. **stride**
   stream

4. The Browns got a _____ to keep them warm. **stamp**
   stove

5. What would you like to _____ with your hot dog? **dress**
   drink

6. Can you see the white _____ on the lake? **swan**
   swing

7. John has a _____ of mud on his pants. **spot**
   strong

8. Look at the _____ climb up the pole! **snake**
   squat

9. When Dad was away, he _____ me a postcard. **sent**
   bent

10. Buy a can of _____ to get rid of the bugs. **sprain**
    spray

11. Mom and Dad want to play _____ on Sunday. **elf**
    golf

12. With the _____ on, no one could tell who she was. **mask**
    task

13. May I keep the _____ I found? **quite**
    quarter

14. We put a _____ over the box to keep in the bug. **screen**
    scream

TEST Initial and final consonant blends

Say each picture name. Circle the letters that stand for the beginning consonant sound. Then write the letters on the line.

1.	2.	3.	4.
_____ (sh) th ch **sh**	_____ ph ch _____ wh	_____ wh th _____ sh	_____ ch ph _____ th

5.	6.	7.	8.
_____ ch th _____ wh	_____ ch sh _____ th	_____ wh sh _____ th	_____ ch sh _____ th

9.	10.	11.	12.
_____ ph th _____ ch	_____ sh ch _____ th	_____ ph th _____ sh	_____ wh th _____ sh

13.	14.	15.	16.
_____ wh sh _____ ch	_____ th ch _____ sh	_____ wh sh _____ ch	_____ sh ch _____ th

Initial consonant digraphs **sh**, **th**, **ch**, **ph**, and **wh**

Say each picture name. Circle the letters that stand for the ending consonant sound. Then write the missing letters.

1.

sh
(th)
ch

th _____

2.

ch _____
sh _____
th _____

3.

sh _____
ch _____
th _____

4.

th _____
ph _____
ch _____

5.

sh _____
ch _____
ph _____

6.

th _____
ch _____
sh _____

7.

ph _____
th _____
sh _____

8.

th _____
ch _____
sh _____

9.

ph _____
th _____
ch _____

10.

sh _____
ch _____
th _____

11.

th _____
ph _____
ch _____

12.

sh _____
ch _____
ph _____

13.

th _____
ph _____
ch _____

14.

ch _____
th _____
sh _____

15.

sh _____
ph _____
th _____

16.

th _____
ph _____
sh _____

Final consonant digraphs **sh**, **th**, **ch**, **ph**, and **wh**

Say each picture name. Circle the word that names the picture.

1.
shade   thing
(whale)   phone

2.
that   thin
shave   chain

3.
shark   photo
where   think

4.
chest   phone
whip   there

5.
chick   dash
graph   bath

6.
ship   thank
this   wheel

7.
graph   dish
bench   with

8.
chest   photo
shine   which

9.
beach   moth
peach   rash

10.
photo   thick
shell   whip

11.
brush   moth
teeth   lunch

12.
graph   path
bunch   bush

13.
cheese   this
chop   shop

14.
dish   peach
then   white

15.
whine   thank
whip   cheek

16.
thumb   shone
chip   shave

Inital and final consonant digraphs **sh**, **th**, **ch**, **ph**, and **wh**   Unit 6/Lesson 39   **107**

Read each sentence. Circle the word that completes the sentence. Then write the word on the line.

1. Please **wash** your face before you go to sleep.   (wash)   with

2. My _____ came out when I was eating my lunch.   tooth   **trash**

3. I _____ Mr. Perez is a very nice man.   shine   **think**

4. In the fall, we like to walk on the _____ around the lake.   push   **path**

5. Do you know how to use the _____ to call for help?   thank   **phone**

6. We like to sit in the shade at the _____.   bush   **beach**

7. I _____ you were here to see the ships.   wish   with

8. For the play, Sarah put a big red dot on her _____.   chin   **thin**

9. I always carry a _____ of my sister.   graph   **photo**

10. Can you tell me _____ road goes west?   why   **which**

11. Maria wants to _____ you for your gift.   **thank**   that

12. Is this the _____ you found on the beach?   wheel   **shell**

13. A big _____ jumped out of the pail.   **fish**   peach

14. My dog likes to play with an old _____.   shoe   thin

Initial and final consonant digraphs **sh, th, ch, ph,** and **wh**

NAME _____

Say each picture name. Circle the letters that stand for the beginning consonant sound. Then write the letters on the line.

1. kn (kn) wr	2. _____ kn wr	3. _____ kn wr	4. _____ kn wr
5. _____ kn wr	6. _____ kn wr	7. _____ kn wr	8. _____ kn wr
9. 2+3=5 _____ kn wr	10. _____ kn wr	11. _____ kn wr	12. _____ kn wr
13. _____ kn wr	14. _____ kn wr	15. _____ kn wr	16. _____ kn wr

Initial consonant digraphs **wr** and **kn**

Read each sentence. Circle the word that completes the sentence. Then write the word on the line.

1. Josh will ___write___ a thank-you note for the gift. (write) wren

2. I saw Kim fall and hurt her right _____. knee kneel

3. Your answer to that question was _____. write wrong

4. Before you come in, please _____ first. knot knock

5. Who made this tight _____ in the rope? know knot

6. Ben helped me _____ the gift. wrap write

7. Use your _____ to cut the meat. knot knife

8. Mr. Carlson did not want to _____ the old homes. wreath wreck

9. Will you put a _____ on your door? wrench wreath

10. I know how to use a _____. wren wrench

11. Turn the _____ to the right and the door will open. knob knit

12. Ms. Golden showed us how to _____ a scarf. knee knit

13. I like to hear a _____ sing. wreck wren

14. The cuff is too big for my _____. wrist wrap

Initial consonant digraphs **wr** and **kn**

Say each picture name. Circle the letters that stand for the ending consonant sound. Then write the letters on the line.

1.	2.	3.	4.
mb tch (dge)	ll ss ff	mb dge ll	ss ll ff
badge	ba___	thu___	cla___

5.	6.	7.	8.
ss tch dge	ff ll ss	mb dge tch	dge tch mb
swi___	cli___	bri___	cru___

9.	10.	11.	12.
ll ss ff	dge tch mb	tch ss ll	dge tch mb
be___	co___	dre___	wa___

13.	14.	15.	16.
ff ll mb	tch dge mb	tch dge ll	mb ll ss
pu___	pa___	ju___	bu___

Final consonant digraphs **mb**, **ss**, **ll**, **ff**, **tch**, and **dge**

Read each sentence. Circle the word that completes the sentence. Then write the word on the line.

1. Take _____off_____ your coat if it gets too hot. all (off)

2. It takes a long time to _____ to the top of the hill. cliff climb

3. I see many cars cross that _____ every day. bridge watch

4. Diane had a bad _____ and hurt her knee. full fall

5. Can you hear the church _____ ring? fall bell

6. The pretty box was made out of blue _____. ball glass

7. I just saw your cat jump over the _____. badge hedge

8. The eggs will _____ in three weeks. hatch match

9. I hope you win the _____ game. puff chess

10. _____ me if you want to go to the show. Comb Call

11. It is not safe to light a _____ near old rags. patch match

12. Your _____ helps you pick up things with your hand. comb thumb

13. Dad put a red knee _____ over the hole. puff patch

14. Will you mend the rip in the _____ of my pants? cuff puff

Final consonant digraphs **mb, ss, ll, ff, tch,** and **dge**

Phonics in Action

Read the story.

Whale Watch

Ruth and Phil meet on the porch.
They hike across the bridge.
Ruth finds the path.
The friends climb up the hill.
They reach the edge.
Phil can watch the whales.
Ruth takes photographs.

Write the word on the line that completes each sentence about the story.

_____

1. Ruth and _____ meet on the porch.

_____

2. They hike across the _____.

_____

3. Phil can watch the _____.

Look at the picture. Find the number and follow the arrow. Write the word on the puzzle.

Across

2. →

3. →

4. →

5. →

Down

1. ↓

3. ↓

REVIEW Beginning and ending consonant digraphs

Say each picture name. Write the letters that stand for the beginning consonant sound.

1. ink	**2.** ip	**3.** ee	**4.** one
5. ob	**6.** ip	**7.** in	**8.** ench
9. igh	**10.** oto	**11.** in	**12.** eel
13. op	**14.** ite	**15.** oe	**16.** alk

Say each picture name. Write the letters that stand for the ending consonant sound.

1. fi___	2. swi___	3. mo___	4. che___
5. fu___	6. pea___	7. cu___	8. gra___
9. too___	10. dre___	11. wa___	12. be___
13. ki___	14. tra___	15. stre___	16. cli___

TEST Final consonant digraphs

When the vowel **a** is followed by the letter **r,** the vowel sound is neither long nor short. It is the vowel sound you hear in the word **car.** Say each picture name. Write **ar** under the picture if the name has this vowel sound.

1. ar ___	2. ___ ___	3. ___ ___	4. ___ ___
5. ___ ___	6. ___ ___	7. ___ ___	8. ___ ___
9. ___ ___	10. ___ ___	11. ___ ___	12. ___ ___
13. ___ ___	14. ___ ___	15. ___ ___	16. ___ ___

Say each picture name. Circle the word that names the picture.

1.	2.	3.	4.
(car) cart cap cape	arm bat bake barn	have hat harp farm	pat dart park pail
5.	6.	7.	8.
cat star shark rake	save sat scarf cart	fan frame farm quart	shark card shave cap
9.	10.	11.	12.
dart van army frail	jab jar jail jam	yak yard whale yarn	car card cap cape
13.	14.	15.	16.
rat quail rail quart	park pail pat part	card cart cave cap	bat army bay arm

When the vowel **o** is followed by the letter **r**, the vowel sound is neither long nor short. It is the vowel sound you hear in the word **corn.** Say each picture name. Write **or** under the picture if the name has this vowel sound.

1.	2.	3.	4.
___ ___ <u>or</u>	___ ___	___ ___	___ ___

5.	6.	7.	8.
___ ___	___ ___	___ ___	___ ___

9.	10.	11.	12.
___ ___	___ ___	___ ___	___ ___

13.	14.	15.	16.
___ ___	___ ___	___ ___	___ ___

Say each picture name. Circle the word that names the picture.

1.	2.	3.	4.
(corn) core cot code	stop stove store stork	fort fork fox frog	hope horse corn hop
5.	6.	7.	8.
shore slot tore soap	pot role fork fort	hole horse hop horn	rope stork rob store
9.	10.	11.	12.
loaf hog stork horse	torn mop torch move	cork cot core cove	hose horse torch toad
13.	14.	15.	16.
core dot cord dome	pot porch tore coal	box bone core bore	port pot porch pole

Say each picture name. Circle the letters that stand for the vowel sound. Then write the letters on the line to complete the word.

1. (or)	2. ar / or	3. ar / or	4. ar / or
_____ corn	__ st __	h __ se	c __ d

5. ar / or	6. ar / or	7. ar / or	8. ar / or
f __ t	b __ n	st __ k	h __ p

9. ar / or	10. ar / or	11. ar / or	12. ar / or
y __ n	h __ n	j __	p __ ch

13. ar / or	14. ar / or	15. ar / or	16. ar / or
c __ t	t __ ch	sh __ k	__ c __

Read each sentence. Circle the word that completes the sentence. Then write the word on the line.

1. In July, Stacy and Steve are going to the _____**shore**_____.

storm
(shore)

2. Kim likes to play in the park when it is _____.

warm
wart

3. Can you reach the _____ on the top shelf?

jar
tar

4. Look at the _____ eating the pile of hay.

horse
porch

5. Miss Coyle will _____ our test next week.

park
mark

6. José and Diane played a game on the _____.

pork
porch

7. Bob placed a _____ next to each dish.

fork
fort

8. Karen will play a song on the _____.

hard
harp

9. We ate some _____ with our ham.

corn
cord

10. A _____ has long legs and a long neck.

store
stork

11. Lisa keeps her horse in a _____.

barn
card

12. Dad will get some milk at the _____.

stork
store

13. Jenny lives on a _____ with her Mom and Dad.

farm
arm

14. Pat will make a cap with the blue _____.

yarn
barn

Ar and or

Say each picture name. Circle the word that names the picture.

1.
feet (fern)
fun turn

2.
clean curb
clerk cub

3.
burn bib
beet bird

4.
shirt shed
ship perch

5.
purse perch
peel pen

6.
curl cup
curb cute

7.
herd hurt
hen heel

8.
twirl first
twin fire

9.
skirt shirt
skip shell

10.
turn meat
burn met

11.
nurse put
purse prune

12.
bird burn
bug bean

13.
herd third
kit kite

14.
churn chute
church chip

15.
girl gem
give germ

16.
fuse nurse
flute rut

Read each sentence. Circle the word that completes the sentence. Then write the word on the line.

1. A ___**fern**___ is a plant that grows in the shade. (fern) burn

2. Donna used a stick to _____ the paint. **fur** **stir**

3. My bird likes to sit on its _____. **purse** **perch**

4. Jerry asked the _____ for his change. **clerk** **germ**

5. A _____ got off the bus with me. **twirl** **girl**

6. Look at the _____ of horses feeding on the oats. **herd** **curl**

7. Rosa put on a green _____ to go to the show. **skirt** **dirt**

8. My father is a _____. **purse** **nurse**

9. Carol came in _____ in the race. **first** **thirst**

10. It is my _____ to ride the bike. **turn** **churn**

11. A _____ uses its wings to fly. **third** **bird**

12. Mom will _____ logs in the stove to keep warm. **burn** **turn**

13. Susan likes to swim and _____ at the shore. **surf** **curb**

14. Tom is the _____ man on the left. **third** **herd**

Er, ir, and ur

Read each word in the box. If the word has the same vowel sound

as 🚗 , write the word in the first column. If the word has the

same vowel sound as 🌽 , write the word in the middle column. If

the word has the same vowel sound as 🪴 , write the word in the
third column.

farm	card	herd	perk	horse	porch
clerk	germ	fork	shark	star	fern
torch	stork	dart	horn	perch	yard

farm

Say each picture name. Circle the letters that stand for the vowel sound. Then write the letters on the line to complete the word.

1. (ar) ir	2. or ur	3. ar ir	4. or ur
c a r t	p __ se	b __ d	f __ t

5. ar ur	6. or ir	7. ar ur	8. or ir
n __ se	c __ d	y __ n	g __ l

9. ir ar	10. ur or	11. ir ar	12. ur or
sh __ k	f __ k	sh __ t	c __ b

13. ur ar	14. ir or	15. ur ar	16. ir or
p __ k	sk __ t	d __ t	h __ n

Phonics in Action

Read the story.

Jordan at Work

Jordan crosses the yard.
He gets his horse from the barn.
They ride out to the herd.
The horse gives a start.
Jordan falls in the dirt.
He hurts his arm.
Jordan finds the nurse.
She makes his arm better.

Write the word on the line that completes each sentence about the story.

1. Jordan gets his _____ from the barn.

2. The horse gives a _____.

3. The _____ makes Jordan's arm better.

Look at the picture. Then read the sentence. Circle the word that
rhymes with the underlined word. Write the word on the line.

	1. It rhymes with <u>yarn</u>. **barn**	(barn) yard harm
	2. It rhymes with <u>force</u>.	mouse nurse horse
	3. It rhymes with <u>dirt</u>.	dart shirt short
	4. It rhymes with <u>farm</u>.	arm hard card
	5. It rhymes with <u>purse</u>.	start horse nurse
	6. It rhymes with <u>yard</u>.	card corn barn

REVIEW **Ar, er, or, ir,** and **ur**

Say each picture name. Write the missing letters on the line.

1. f _ n	2. p _ k	3. _ c _ b	4. p _ ch
5. d _ k	6. b _ n	7. sk _ t	8. f _ k
9. p _ se	10. sh _ t	11. c _ t	12. g _ l
13. sc _ f	14. h _ n	15. n _ se	16. c _ d

Read each sentence. Circle the word that completes the sentence. Then
write the word on the line.

1. Susan is the _____ girl on the team. **third**
   bird

2. Mr. Jackson asked us to _____ our seats around. **burn**
   turn

3. It was kind of Jenny to send a birthday _____. **cork**
   card

4. Laura left the box with _____ mother. **her**
   fur

5. Watch the _____ fly to its perch. **born**
   bird

6. The _____ sent me home when I was sick. **purse**
   nurse

7. My new _____ has red and blue stripes. **scarf**
   shark

8. Anita works very _____ at her new job. **hard**
   harp

9. Dad works as a _____ in the store. **chirp**
   clerk

10. We do not _____ our trash. **burn**
    bird

11. A thick string or a thin rope is called a _____. **cord**
    cart

12. The storm did little _____ to the crops. **hark**
    harm

13. Luis wore a blue _____ to the show. **shirt**
    hurt

14. We saw a _____ of smoke over our home. **cure**
    curl

Say the name of the picture in each box. Circle the pictures with names that have the same vowel sound as the picture in the box.

The vowel letters **oo** can stand for the vowel sound you hear in the word **book** or the vowel sound you hear in the word **moon.** Say each picture name. Circle the word that names the picture.

1.	2.	3.	4.
cook (book) hood pool	stool pool spool school	broom roof room root	book brook look cook

5.	6.	7.	8.
loose goose moose tooth	fool spoon stool spool	hood hoof soot boot	mood foot wood food

9.	10.	11.	12.
broom moon room groom	boot goose moose foot	boom broom boot book	roof hoof root hood

13.	14.	15.	16.
school pool stool stood	food hood took hook	loose tooth booth look	too root zoo roof

Say the name each large picture. If the picture has the same vowel sound you hear in the word **book**, circle the book. If the picture name has the same vowel sound you hear in the word **moon**, circle the moon. Then write the name of the large picture on the line.

1.	2.	3.	4.
wood			

5.	6.	7.	8.

9.	10.	11.	12.

13.	14.	15.	16.

Read each sentence. Circle the word that completes the sentence. Then write the word on the line.

1. When it is hot, I like to swim in the ___ pool ___. (pool) stool

2. Tom will chop the _____ for the fire. **hood** **wood**

3. Please put your coat on the first _____. **hook** **look**

4. Rosa read a _____ about a moose. **book** **took**

5. John put his _____ over his head. **stood** **hood**

6. The soft hair of a sheep is called _____. **wool** **wood**

7. Mom and I went fishing in the _____. **brook** **broom**

8. Mark called me from a phone _____. **moose** **booth**

9. The _____ of red thread is on the shelf. **spool** **spoon**

10. Our class went to the _____ on Monday. **zoo** **too**

11. It is too _____ to eat on the porch. **pool** **cool**

12. Did you _____ in the car for the map? **look** **cook**

13. My _____ has a swing and slide in the yard. **school** **spool**

14. Which _____ will you use to fix the van? **took** **tool**

Say each picture name. Color the picture orange if its name has the same vowel sound as the word **cow.** Color the picture blue if its name has the same vowel sound as the word **boy.**

1.
2.
3.
4.
5.
6.
7.
8.
9.
10.
11.
12.
13.
14.
15.
16.

Diphthongs **ow** and **oy**

The letters **ow** can stand for the vowel sound you hear in the word **cow.** The letters **oy** stand for the vowel sound you hear in the word **boy.** Say each picture name. Circle the word that names the picture.

1. now **boy** / toy gown
2. clown joy / toy owl
3. coy joy / power flowers
4. now town / cow frown
5. frown town / owl growl
6. plow coy / flower Roy
7. down frown / plow clown
8. toy vowels / Roy gown
9. joy crown / gown Roy
10. plow coy / brow toys
11. clown brown / town gown
12. plow fowl / growl owl
13. down frown / gown brown
14. now gown / bow vowels
15. crowd gown / down boy
16. brown clown / brow town

Diphthongs **ow** and **oy**

Say each picture name. Write the letters that stand for the vowel sound.

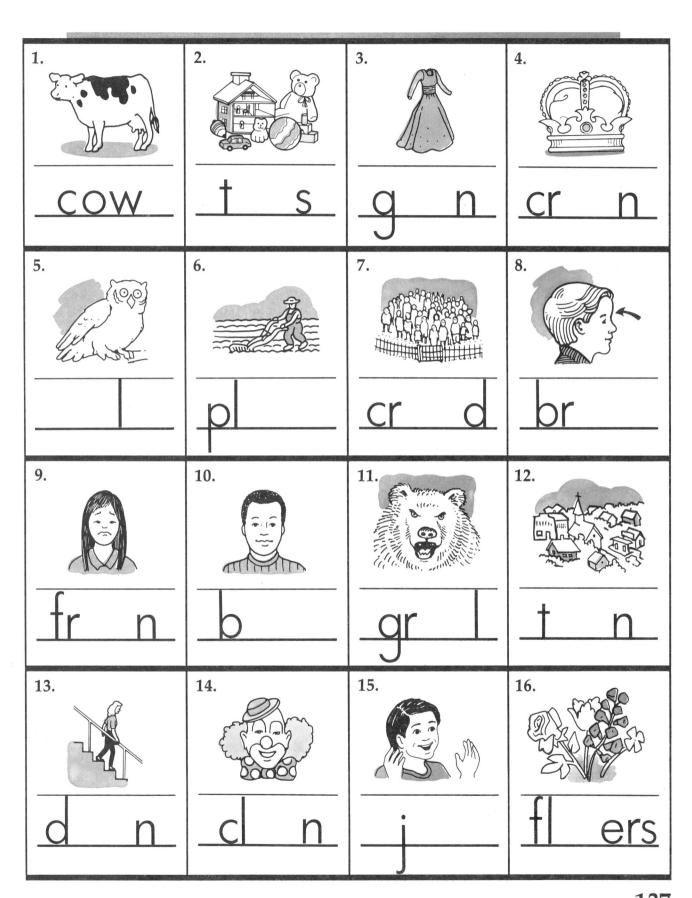

1. cow

2. t___s

3. g___n

4. cr___n

5. ___l

6. pl___

7. cr___d

8. br___

9. fr___n

10. b___

11. gr___l

12. t___n

13. d___n

14. cl___n

15. j___

16. fl___ers

Read each sentence. Circle the word that completes the sentence. Then
write the word on the line.

1. Can that ___**boy**___ play the drum? (**boy**) **brown**

2. The queen wears a _____ on her head. **town** **crown**

3. My new coat is white and _____. **brow** **brown**

4. _____ is coming to my home on Wednesday. **Roy** **Town**

5. A _____ is a tool used in farming. **plow** **growl**

6. Did you see the _____ eat the pile of hay? **down** **cow**

7. There will be a big _____ at the ball game. **crowd** **enjoy**

8. The red or white rose is a pretty _____. **frown** **flower**

9. We _____ toast and eggs for breakfast. **growl** **enjoy**

10. My sister looked very pretty in her blue _____. **gown** **frown**

11. After the race there was sweat on my _____. **town** **brow**

12. The _____ car has a red hood. **toy** **gown**

13. In which _____ does Roberto live? **town** **frown**

14. My dog will _____ when it sees a cat. **growl** **owl**

Say each picture name. Circle the word that names the picture.

1.	2.	3.	4.
(cook) book look took	crowd clown crown gown	stool school spoon spool	joy Roy boy toys
5.	6.	7.	8.
brow growl down frown	tooth moose loose goose	how plow now cow	food good wood book
9.	10.	11.	12.
zoo too noon moon	growl frown owl gown	brook broom book boom	town down gown crown
13.	14.	15.	16.
boy toy crowd brown	soot boot roof root	shoot hood spool school	Roy crowd toy town

Read each sentence. Circle the word that completes the sentence. Then write the word on the line.

1. The king put a ___crown___ on his head.   **gown** (**crown**)

2. Rosa _____ her books to school.   **took** **look**

3. Tracy let me play with her new _____.   **toy** **brow**

4. Please use the _____ to clean the floor.   **brook** **broom**

5. Tonight there will be a full _____.   **moon** **spoon**

6. Bill fell _____ and hurt his arm.   **down** **frown**

7. The new _____ in our class has a pet snake.   **brow** **boy**

8. A _____ is a bird that can swim.   **moose** **goose**

9. The _____ had on a tiny hat and a huge coat.   **clown** **brown**

10. _____ will be seven on Tuesday.   **Roy** **Toys**

11. We saw the seals and the apes at the _____.   **zoo** **zoom**

12. My best friend is going to move to a new _____.   **bow** **town**

13. Pam likes to play ball and swim _____.   **food** **too**

14. Joe had a _____ on his face after he lost his hat.   **frown** **gown**

REVIEW Diphthongs **oo** (book), **oo** (moon), **ow**, and **oy**

Say each picture name. Color the picture orange if its name has the same vowel sound as the word **house.** Color the picture blue if its name has the same vowel sound as the word **soil.**

1.

2.

3.

4.

5.

6.

7.

8.

9.

10.

11.

12.

13.

14.

15.

16.

The letters **ou** stand for the vowel sound you hear in the word **house**.
The letters **oi** stand for the vowel sound you hear in the word **soil**.
Circle the word that names the picture.

1. (boil) broil blouse house	**2.** trout shout spout scout	**3.** bounce noise count mount	**4.** soil coil south coins
5. snout cloud shout noise	**6.** count pouch scout moist	**7.** pound couch pouch point	**8.** blouse noise hound join
9. pouch broil couch foil	**10.** moist mouse mouth mount	**11.** loud snout proud shout	**12.** couch coins mouse coil
13. house mouth mouse point	**14.** join spoil hound oil	**15.** sound coins round joins	**16.** point moist pouch mouth

Diphthongs **ou** and **oi**

Say each picture name. Write the letters that stand for the vowel
sound on the line.

1.	2.	3.	4.
b <u>oi</u> l	m <u> </u> th	<u> </u> l	c <u> </u> ch
5.	6.	7.	8.
m <u> </u> se	c <u> </u> ns	sn <u> </u> t	bl <u> </u> se
9.	10.	11.	12.
p <u> </u> nt	cl <u> </u> d	br <u> </u> l	p <u> </u> ch
13.	14.	15.	16.
s <u> </u> l	sh <u> </u> t	c <u> </u> nt	n <u> </u> se

Read each sentence. Circle the word that completes the sentence. Then write the word on the line.

1. Do you know how to __mount__ a horse? (mount) shout

2. Wrap the ham in _____ and put it away. foil coil

3. We need to buy gas and _____ in the next town. boil oil

4. I hope that the rain will not _____ the game. spoil soil

5. When it gets cold, many birds fly _____. mouth south

6. My new pin has a sharp _____. point joint

7. The _____ in my yard is good for plants. soil boil

8. We have to _____ hands for this dance. coin join

9. Bob was taking a nap on the blue _____. couch pouch

10. There is not one _____ in the sky today. loud cloud

11. Spray the plants each week to keep them _____. moist noise

12. The little _____ climbed up the steps. house mouse

13. When you drop a ball, it will _____. bounce ounce

14. A cent or a dime is a kind of _____. join coin

Say each picture name. Circle the word that names the picture.

1.

(couch) cow
pouch plow

2.

boil boy
broil toy

3.

count crown
bounce brown

4.

stool hood
spool hook

5.

toys coins
boys joins

6.

look broom
moon brook

7.

frown gown
scout shout

8.

toys point
boys coil

9.

crowd proud
growl loud

10.

goose loose
tooth moose

11.

could hood
snout shout

12.

boy soil
foil boil

13.

house how
mouse brow

14.

soil boy
oil toy

15.

now out
plow shout

16.

spoon loose
stool goose

Read each sentence. Circle the word that completes the sentence. Then write the word on the line.

1. Dad will __broil__ the fish for our meal. (broil) **broom**

2. The _____ on this pin is very sharp. **plow point**

3. My dog comes _____ the road every day to meet me. **down frown**

4. Pat _____ very still for her photo. **stood hood**

5. Jim will _____ for help. **shout soil**

6. Judy wore her new red _____ to school. **blouse mouse**

7. Look at the vine _____ around the tree. **coil boil**

8. Rose will buy a new _____ for her brother Luis. **toy join**

9. A _____ is a bird that looks like a duck. **moose goose**

10. My little sister can _____ from one to ten. **count couch**

11. Our class is going to the _____ on Friday. **zoo tooth**

12. The _____ is the front part of a ship. **brow bow**

13. My new book is a _____ to read. **boy joy**

14. Spring will be here _____. **soon look**

REVIEW Diphthongs **oo** (book), **oo** (moon), **ow, oy, ou,** and **oi**

Say each picture name. Circle the picture if the name has the same
vowel sound as the word **claw**.

1.	2.	3.	4.
5.	6.	7.	8.
9.	10.	11.	12.
13.	14.	15.	16.

The letters **au, aw,** and **al** stand for the same vowel sound. It is the vowel sound you hear in the words **sauce, claw,** and **salt.** Circle the word that names the picture.

1.	**2.**	**3.**	**4.**
pause fault (claw) caught	bald salt halt jaw	haul sauce hawk auto	fawn yawn crawl lawn
5.	**6.**	**7.**	**8.**
false fault salt halt	straw pause paw draw	taught yawn fault fawn	chalk haul sauce squawk
9.	**10.**	**11.**	**12.**
chalk thaw claw straw	cause false haul caught	hawk squawk lawn shawl	paw vault yawn hawk
13.	**14.**	**15.**	**16.**
raw saw claw straw	drawn stalk lawn false	hawk chalk halt thaw	thaw draw false jaw

Vowel combinations **au, aw,** and **al**

Say each picture name. Circle the letters that stand for the vowel sound. Then write the letters on the line to complete the word.

1. (aw) oo	**2.** al oo	**3.** aw oo	**4.** au oo
claw	s t	sh l	h d
5. al oo	**6.** aw oy	**7.** au ow	**8.** al ow
ch k	b	s ce	b d
9. au ou	**10.** aw oi	**11.** au ou	**12.** aw oi
h se	str	to	s
13. aw oo	**14.** au ow	**15.** aw oy	**16.** aw oi
l n	cr n	h k	y n

Vowel combinations **au**, **aw**, and **al**

Read each sentence. Circle the word that completes the sentence. Then write the word on the line.

1. Paul is drinking his milk with a ___straw___ . (straw) lawn

2. A _____ is a baby deer. fawn hawk

3. Sue helped her dad cut the green _____. bald lawn

4. Tom had to _____ before he could walk. crawl shawl

5. You are right, it is my _____. fault pause

6. Ellen saw a _____ flying in the sky. chalk hawk

7. Pam and I _____ two big fish today. caught dawn

8. We plan to start on our trip at _____. cause dawn

9. Dad told me to use less _____ on my food. salt bald

10. Carla and Bob used a _____ to cut the wood. saw paw

11. Can I help _____ away the rocks? auto haul

12. The ice should _____ now that it is warm. thaw claw

13. The game came to a _____ when it started to rain. halt false

14. Would you like some _____ on your meat? shawl sauce

Vowel combinations au, aw, and al

The letters **ew** can stand for the vowel sound you hear in the word **chew**. The letters **ow** can stand for the vowel sound you hear in the word **snow**. Say each picture name. Circle the word that names the picture.

1.	2.	3.	4.
flew grew (snow) grow	low tow drew knew	chew blew know glow	threw grew slow bowl

5.	6.	7.	8.
tow crow blew chew	screw threw crow blow	crew grew low bow	grow throw screw stew

9.	10.	11.	12.
flew drew blow flow	mow row crew drew	snow show stew grew	flow show drew grew

13.	14.	15.	16.
grew threw blow bowl	screw threw row tow	stew screw flow glow	flew drew slow blow

Read each sentence. Circle the word that completes the sentence. Then write the word on the line.

1. Karen likes to ride her sled in the __snow__. flow (snow)

2. Jill _____ the ball to Steve.   threw grew

3. John is going to _____ me his new bike.   show glow

4. Would you please _____ a new bulb into the lamp?   grew screw

5. Rosa will _____ the boat across the lake.   row bowl

6. The bat _____ into the dark cave.   flew knew

7. Mom made a _____ of beef and rice.   crew stew

8. Do you _____ how to fix the TV?   know grow

9. Bill put a red _____ on the gift box.   bow tow

10. José has a _____ of soup for lunch.   bowl show

11. My dog likes to _____ on an old bone.   drew chew

12. Judy will _____ the lawn on Saturday.   slow mow

13. The truck will _____ the car back to our home.   tow crow

14. The wind _____ all last night.   blew drew

Diphthongs **ew** and **ow**

Say each picture name. Circle the word that names the picture.

1.

clown   scout
crown   shout

2.

cook   brook
look   shook

3.

shawl   chalk
haul   talk

4.

frown   house
gown   mouse

5.

stool   tool
fool   pool

6.

false   straw
claw   thaw

7.

wood   good
stood   hood

8.

mow   row
crew   drew

9.

joy   oil
boy   boil

10.

noise   toys
coin   joy

11.

owl   pouch
plow   mouth

12.

salt   yawn
fault   fawn

13.

sauce   halt
squawk   fault

14.

growl   snout
owl   shout

15.

soil   Roy
foil   toy

16.

drew   flew
slow   blow

Read each sentence. Circle the word that completes the sentence. Then write the word on the line.

1. Kevin ate his ice cream with a large __spoon__.   spool ⟨spoon⟩

2. Do you _____ the way to the mall?   know throw

3. We _____ the kite above our house.   drew flew

4. Mom will buy a new _____ on Friday.   haul auto

5. We use very little _____ on our food.   salt halt

6. The plane made a lot of _____ when it took off.   noise mouse

7. There was a dark _____ in the sky before the storm.   cloud loud

8. Laura put the mail in the mail _____.   couch pouch

9. Class will start as _____ as we take our seats.   soon room

10. My cat likes to _____ under the fence.   crawl shawl

11. This _____ is good for planting seeds.   soil boil

12. My new scarf has _____ and white stripes.   clown brown

13. Would you like me to get you a new _____?   joy toy

14. Diane cuts the _____ every Saturday.   lawn dawn

Phonics in Action

Read the story.

The Loose Moose

Dawn and Roy go to the town zoo.
They see a brown hawk chew.
Dawn looks at a big round goose.
Roy sees a moose get loose.
They join a crowd.
The noise is loud.
Some boys point and people shout.
They see the one that just got out.

Write the word on the line that completes each sentence about the story.

_____

1. Dawn and Roy see a hawk _____.

_____

2. Roy sees a _____ gets loose.

_____

3. Some boys _____ at the moose.

Look at the picture. Then read the sentence. Circle the word that
rhymes with the underlined word. Write the word on the line.

1.

It rhymes with look. __book__

(book)
like
moon

2.

It rhymes with out. _____

sheet
oat
shout

3.

It rhymes with loose. _____

goose
lease
mouse

4.

It rhymes with growl. _____

grow
bowl
owl

5.

It rhymes with squawk. _____

hawk
hack
took

6.

It rhymes with chew. _____

grow
stew
stow

Say each picture name. Circle the letters that stand for the vowel
sound. Then write the letters on the line.

1. oi ou aw c l o u d	**2.** ow aw ew ch	**3.** oi aw ow sh l	**4.** oi ow oy g n
5. ou oo oi b l	**6.** oo oi ou br k	**7.** oo oy aw t s	**8.** aw ow ew scr
9. oi aw ow l n	**10.** oi ou ew p nt	**11.** ou oo al ch k	**12.** ou ow au s ce
13. aw ow ew m	**14.** ow oy aw thr	**15.** ou oi oo st l	**16.** oo oi ou bl se

Read each sentence. Circle the word that completes the sentence. Then write the word on the line.

1. I keep my books on a _____ shelf. **low** **glow**

2. A _____ has a long, thin tail. **mouse** **house**

3. Maria is going to buy a _____ car in April. **chew** **new**

4. The farmer knows how to _____ the field. **now** **plow**

5. The _____ of my new pin is very sharp. **point** **join**

6. Roy needs a _____ of meat for the stew. **sound** **pound**

7. We saw a _____ about fish on TV last night. **show** **slow**

8. Lois is drinking her milk with a _____. **sauce** **straw**

9. My _____ is on the next street. **school** **moon**

10. The fire chief will _____ to our class next week. **talk** **chalk**

11. You use your _____ to speak and sing. **soil** **voice**

12. We saw the polar bears and the snakes at the _____. **zoo** **too**

13. Which _____ do you like the most? **joy** **toy**

14. Mother and I painted my _____ green. **room** **boom**

158 Unit 8/Lesson 59   TEST Diphthongs and vowel combinations

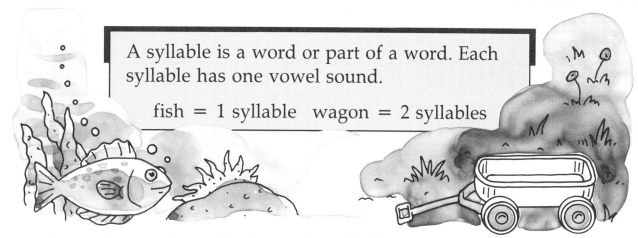

A syllable is a word or part of a word. Each syllable has one vowel sound.

fish = 1 syllable   wagon = 2 syllables

Say each picture name. Listen for the number of syllables, or word parts. Write the number of syllables in each word.

1.	2.	3.	4.	5.
1	___	___	___	___

6.	7.	8.	9.	10.
___	___	___	___	___

11.	12.	13.	14.	15.
___	___	___	___	___

A compound word is a word made up of two words. Divide a compound word between the two words.

birdhouse   bird / house

Read each compound word. Draw a line between the two words that make up the compound word.

1. sea/shell
2. steamboat
3. sidewalk
4. bathrobe
5. playpen
6. campfire
7. doorbell
8. airplane
9. necktie
10. bluebird
11. bathroom
12. moonlight
13. pancake
14. toothbrush
15. oatmeal
16. snowstorm
17. notebook
18. dustpan
19. daybreak
20. thumbtack
21. snowball
22. wishbone
23. driveway
24. mailbox
25. cupcake
26. backbone
27. cowhand
28. windshield
29. playground
30. seaweed
31. rainbow
32. baseball
33. doorknob
34. handshake
35. necklace
36. railroad
37. raincoat
38. birthday
39. starfish
40. sunshine
41. wristwatch
42. rainstorm
43. doughnut
44. hillside

Compound words

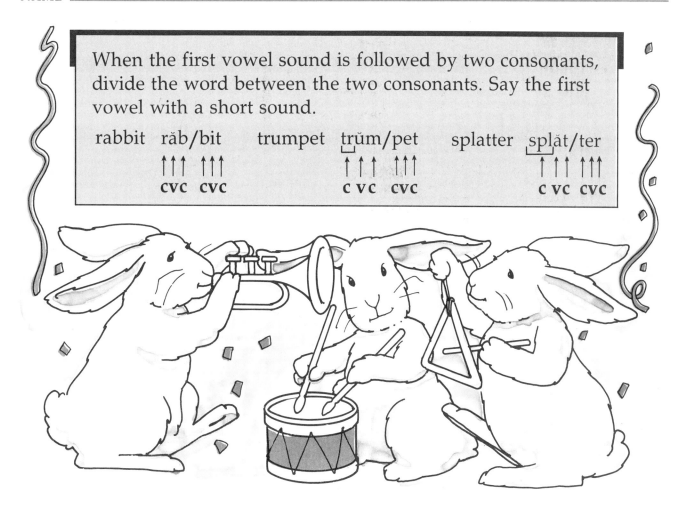

When the first vowel sound is followed by two consonants, divide the word between the two consonants. Say the first vowel with a short sound.

rabbit   răb/bit   trumpet   trŭm/pet   splatter   splăt/ter

↑↑↑ ↑↑↑   ↑↑↑ ↑↑↑   ↑↑↑ ↑↑↑

cvc cvc   c vc cvc   c vc cvc

Read each two-syllable word. Draw a line between the first and second syllables. Then mark the vowel letter in the first syllable with a ˘ to show that it is said with a short sound.

1. yĕl/low
2. button
3. lesson
4. lumber
5. silver
6. kitten
7. velvet
8. thunder
9. finger
10. ladder
11. chatter
12. winter
13. doctor
14. sister
15. pillow
16. bonnet
17. problem
18. dentist
19. skillet
20. pretzel
21. picnic
22. dinner
23. contest
24. helmet
25. magnet
26. muffin
27. whisper
28. number
29. tunnel
30. blanket
31. puppet
32. butter
33. center
34. scamper
35. signal
36. manner
37. pepper
38. letter
39. napkin
40. candy
41. hammer
42. pencil
43. basket
44. zipper

Read each sentence. Circle the word that completes the sentence. Then write the word on the line.

1. My red blanket keeps me very warm. pillow / (blanket)

2. We want to go on a _____ in the woods. picnic / tunnel

3. Hal goes to a _____ when he has a toothache. dentist / helmet

4. Look at the smoke coming from the _____. pencil / chimney

5. Today I wrote a long _____ to my friend Bobby. letter / lesson

6. You can see the ballpark from the _____. window / zipper

7. My dad took the _____ out of my toe. splinter / finger

8. Will you please help me with my math _____? problem / button

9. My dog does not like the sound of _____. thunder / dinner

10. Wait for a green _____ before you cross the street. walrus / signal

11. Linda will put on a _____ show for her friends. puppet / basket

12. Many birds will fly south for the _____. winter / contest

13. Luis has peanut _____ on bread for lunch. butter / muffin

14. Barbara used a _____ and nails to make a toy box. hammer / pretzel

162 Unit 9/Lesson 61

When the first vowel sound is followed by one consonant or consonant sound, try dividing the word before the consonant. Say the first vowel with a long sound.

tiger   tī/ger   spider   spī/der

cv cvc   c v cvc

Read each two-syllable word. Draw a line between the first and second syllables. Then mark the vowel letter in the first syllable with a ⁻ to show that it is said with a long sound.

1. pī/lot
2. paper
3. minus
4. human
5. basin
6. frozen
7. label
8. cider
9. student
10. favor
11. flavor
12. major
13. hotel
14. moment
15. clover
16. pupil
17. fever
18. final
19. silent
20. robot
21. motor
22. begin
23. razor
24. labor
25. total
26. humor
27. bacon
28. meter
29. siren
30. music

Read each sentence. Circle the word that completes the sentence. Then write the word on the line.

1. My mom will ___label___ the fruit she cans. rumor (label)

2. We will grill cheese and _____ for lunch. **bacon** **cider**

3. There is a big _____ bush in our back yard. **silent** **lilac**

4. Fifteen _____ five is ten. **minus** **major**

5. The _____ can fix all our old toys. **robot** **razor**

6. When I go to the zoo, I will first see the _____. **tiger** **basin**

7. We want to ice skate on the _____ pond. **final** **frozen**

8. The _____ will fly the plane when the storm ends. **pilot** **paper**

9. Sam will buy a new _____ for his van. **motor** **moment**

10. We could hear the loud _____ of the fire truck. **flavor** **siren**

11. Did Gloria put a coin in the _____? **meter** **tulip**

12. Would you like a _____ bear for a pet? **polar** **clover**

13. Please take the _____ off my desk. **spider** **total**

14. Kim snaps her fingers to keep time with the _____. **music** **fever**

When the first vowel sound is followed by one consonant or consonant sound, try dividing the word after the consonant. Say the first vowel sound with a short sound.

camel căm/el   dragon drăg/on
       ↑↑↑ ↑↑   ↑↑↑ ↑↑
       cvc vc   c vc vc

Read each two-syllable word. Draw a line between the first and second syllables. Then mark the vowel in the first syllable with a ˘ to show that it is said with a short sound.

1. wăg/on
2. petal
3. timid
4. habit
5. never
6. medal
7. pedal
8. travel
9. punish
10. magic
11. salad
12. clever
13. cabin
14. planet
15. metal
16. lemon
17. medic
18. finish
19. shadow
20. visit
21. model
22. spinach
23. tonic
24. second
25. denim
26. honest
27. solid
28. robin
29. melon
30. seven

Read each sentence. Circle the word that completes the sentence. Then write the word on the line.

1. The winner is the first to cross the **finish** line.
   medal
   (finish)

2. We always put our games on the _____ shelf.
   camel
   metal

3. Joan made a _____ plane for the contest.
   model
   pedal

4. I like to squeeze _____ on fish.
   lemon
   spinach

5. It is fun to box with your _____.
   shadow
   tonic

6. John eats a big green _____ every day.
   salad
   petal

7. Roberto and Steve come to _____ me every Sunday.
   clever
   visit

8. Chris does not want a _____ muffin.
   second
   honest

9. My sister gave me _____ pants for my birthday.
   denim
   planet

10. We saw a _____ show at the circus.
    magic
    never

11. There is a baby _____ on the window sill.
    robin
    travel

12. Will you give me a ride in your _____?
    wagon
    melon

13. The story is about a _____ who sprays fire from its nose.
    dragon
    river

14. When we go to the woods, we stay in an old _____.
    cabin
    gravel

166 Unit 9/Lesson 63

Syllable pattern cvc/vc

Read each two-syllable word. Draw a line between the first and second syllables. Then mark the vowel letter in the first syllable with a ˘ if it is said with a short sound or with a ¯ if it is said with a long sound.

1. zĭp/per
2. fever
3. melon
4. major
5. trumpet
6. punish
7. planet
8. tonic
9. candy
10. window
11. cider
12. flavor
13. music
14. manner
15. medal
16. cabin
17. pedal
18. midget
19. lumber
20. basin
21. label
22. kennel
23. pretzel
24. contest
25. wagon
26. dragon
27. scamper
28. tunnel
29. paper
30. total
31. student
32. river
33. shadow
34. habit
35. travel
36. helmet
37. doctor
38. moment
39. begin
40. velvet
41. slender
42. whisper
43. finish
44. spinach
45. silent
46. cactus
47. bacon
48. bonus
49. denim
50. level
51. solid
52. medic
53. tulip
54. napkin
55. clover
56. puppet
57. button
58. rabbit
59. camel
60. razor

NAME _____

Read each sentence. Circle the word that completes the sentence. Then
write the word on the line.

1. My kitten's fur is as smooth as _____.   velvet
                                                        cactus

2. Alex likes to drink cold apple _____.   cider
                                                      bacon

3. One day I will travel to a far-away _____.   planet
                                                           helmet

4. Can you see the train in the dark _____?   tunnel
                                                         napkin

5. I like the _____ Sal plays on his trumpet.   music
                                                           clover

6. Please put the toy blocks in the red _____.   wagon
                                                            puppet

7. Spot found the lost _____ under the bed.   fever
                                                         button

8. Two tugboats are pulling a barge up the _____.   pretzel
                                                               river

9. We have many _____ plants in our garden.   tulip
                                                         bonus

10. Mom always reads the _____ after dinner.   paper
                                                          trumpet

11. At camp we sleep in a _____ near a big lake.   cabin
                                                             wallet

12. The winner of the _____ will get a gold medal.   contest
                                                               punish

13. My brother drew a picture of a _____.   dragon
                                                       moment

14. Your foot has to reach the _____ to ride a bike.   pedal
                                                                 target

TEST Syllable patterns

When a word ends in a single consonant and the vowel sound is short, double the consonant before adding **ed** or **ing**. There is no spelling change when adding **s**.

scrub scrubb**ed** scrubb**ing** scrub**s**

Read each word listed below. Add the endings **s, ed,** and **ing** to each word. Then write the words on the lines.

	s	ed	ing
1. flap	flaps	flapped	flapping
2. hum			
3. snow			
4. tag			
5. trim			
6. rain			
7. clap			
8. stop			
9. peel			

> When a word ends in a single consonant and the vowel sound is short, double the consonant before adding **er** or **est**.
>
> big   bigg**er**   bigg**est**

Read each word listed below. Add the endings **er** and **est** to each word. Then write the words on the lines.

	er	**est**
1. sad	sadder	saddest
2. thin		
3. flat		
4. neat		
5. slow		
6. red		
7. hot		
8. small		
9. weak		
10. dim		

When a word ends in silent **e**, drop the **e** before **adding ed** or **ing**. There is no spelling change when adding **s**.

dance dance**s** danc**ed** danc**ing**

Read each word listed below. Add the endings **s, ed,** and **ing** to each word. Then write the words on the lines.

	s	**ed**	**ing**
1. like	likes	liked	liking
2. care			
3. jump			
4. love			
5. change			
6. clean			
7. vote			
8. visit			
9. decide			
10. explode			
11. move			

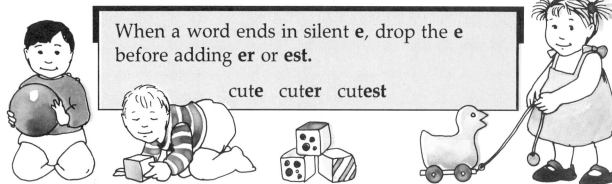

When a word ends in silent **e**, drop the **e** before adding **er** or **est**.

cute   cut**er**   cut**est**

Read each word listed below. Add the endings **er** and **est** to each word. Then write the words on the lines.

	er	est
1. large	larger	largest
2. wise		
3. nice		
4. white		
5. blue		
6. pale		
7. strong		
8. quiet		
9. pure		
10. fine		
11. ripe		

Inflectional endings **er** and **est**

Read each sentence. Add the ending **s, ed, ing, er,** or **est** to each word to complete the sentence. Then write the word on the line. You may need to make spelling changes.

1. Of all the pillows, the green one is the ___nicest___. **(nice + est)**

2. Dad and I _____ the hedges this morning. **(trim + ed)**

3. We need a _____ chest for our books and toys. **(big + er)**

4. The birds in the sky are _____ their wings. **(flap + ing)**

5. My grandmother _____ this sweater for me. **(knit + ed)**

6. This rocking chair _____ when you rock in it. **(squeak + s)**

7. My cheese sandwich is _____ than yours. **(thin + er)**

8. The mattress on my bed is _____. **(sag + ing)**

9. This is the _____ day of the whole summer. **(hot + est)**

10. An orange is much _____ than a lemon. **(sweet + er)**

11. My brother _____ the shiny apple for me. **(peel + ed)**

12. Howie _____ the kitchen floor every night. **(scrub + s)**

13. Cars and trucks are _____ at the red light. **(stop + ed)**

14. This is the _____ leg of the table. **(weak + est)**

Read each sentence. Add the ending **s, ed, ing, er,** or **est** to each word
to complete the sentence. Then write the word on the line. You may
need to make spelling changes.

1. Anita has _larger_ eyes than her sister. **(large + er)**

2. Bumper is the _____ of the six puppies. **(cute + est)**

3. We _____ our sleds to slide down the hill. **(use + ed)**

4. Your yellow shirt is _____ than mine. **(pale + er)**

5. Joey _____ his jacket three times today. **(change + ed)**

6. Carmen _____ the most at the party. **(dance + ed)**

7. This is the _____ board I could find. **(narrow + est)**

8. The reddest apple in the bowl is the _____. **(ripe + est)**

9. I like to hear popcorn _____ in the pot. **(explode + ing)**

10. My brother is _____ his games to my room. **(move + ing)**

11. Ms. Jones is the _____ coach in our school. **(fine + est)**

12. Andy _____ for the bird with a broken wing. **(care + ed)**

13. Mom and Bobby _____ out the garage. **(clean + ed)**

14. Amy is ice _____ on the pond. **(skate + ing)**

When a word ends in **y** with a consonant before it, change the **y** to **i** before adding **es** to make the word plural, or mean more than one.

pony   pon**ies**

Read each word listed below. Add the ending **s** or **es** to each word to make it plural, or mean more than one. Then write the word on the line.

1. berry   berries

2. lady   _____

3. spy   _____

4. city   _____

5. day   _____

6. cherry   _____

7. party   _____

8. daisy   _____

9. supply   _____

10. key   _____

11. cry   _____

12. baby   _____

13. boy   _____

14. penny   _____

15. body   _____

16. buddy   _____

17. army   _____

18. worry   _____

19. monkey   _____

20. valley   _____

21. country   _____

22. ferry   _____

23. chimney   _____

24. donkey   _____

When a word ends in **y** with a consonant before it, change the **y** to **i** before adding **es** or **ed**. There is no spelling change when adding **ing**.

study studi**es** studi**ed** study**ing**

Read each word listed below. Add the endings **s**, **es**, **ed**, or **ing** to each word. Then write the words on the lines.

	s or es	ed	ing
1. cry	cries	cried	crying
2. carry			
3. spray			
4. try			
5. obey			
6. fry			
7. play			
8. copy			
9. hurry			
10. dry			

Inflectional endings **es**, **ed**, and **ing**

> When a word ends in **y** with a consonant before it, change the **y** to **i** before adding **er** or **est**.
>
> tiny   tin**ier**   tin**iest**

Read each word listed below. Add the endings **er** and **est** to each word. Then write the words on the lines.

	er	est
1. silly	sillier	silliest
2. easy		
3. happy		
4. steady		
5. lucky		
6. funny		
7. heavy		
8. lazy		
9. early		
10. busy		
11. dirty		
12. muddy		

Read each sentence. Add the ending **s, es, ed, ing, er,** or **est** to each word to complete the sentences. Then write the word on the line. You may need to make spelling changes.

1. That is the __spookiest__ house on the block. **(spooky + est)**

2. I always get up _____ on school days. **(early + er)**

3. We saw white and yellow _____ in the fields. **(daisy + es)**

4. Checkers is the _____ moving turtle I know. **(slow + est)**

5. We _____ out the door to catch the bus. **(hurry + ed)**

6. Campers can buy food _____ at that store. **(supply + es)**

7. Brian told the _____ joke at the birthday party. **(silly + est)**

8. Our team is _____ to win the track medal. **(try + ing)**

9. Josh is going to three _____ next month. **(party + es)**

10. My baby brother _____ when he is hungry. **(cry + es)**

11. Kara got a _____ score than I on the math test. **(high + er)**

12. The car _____ are on the counter in the kitchen. **(key + s)**

13. Lynn saved _____ and quarters for new skates. **(penny + es)**

14. March has the _____ days of the whole year. **(windy + est)**

REVIEW Inflectional endings **s, es, ed, ing, er,** and **est**

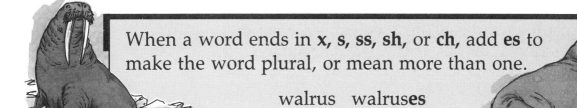

When a word ends in **x, s, ss, sh,** or **ch,** add **es** to make the word plural, or mean more than one.

walrus   walrus**es**

Read each word listed below. Add the ending **s** or **es** to each word to make it plural, or mean more than one. Then write the word on the line.

1. wish   _wishes_

2. glass   _____

3. flag   _____

4. star   _____

5. porch   _____

6. patch   _____

7. compass   _____

8. robot   _____

9. torch   _____

10. mix   _____

11. shark   _____

12. ostrich   _____

13. pumpkin   _____

14. sandwich   _____

15. guess   _____

16. wax   _____

17. beaver   _____

18. broom   _____

19. bush   _____

20. dress   _____

21. six   _____

22. bus   _____

23. tax   _____

24. gas   _____

Inflectional ending **s** and **es**

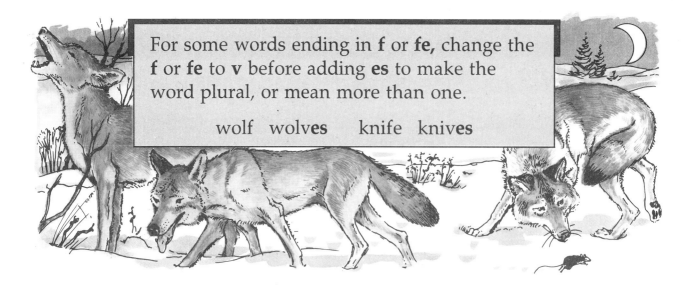

For some words ending in **f** or **fe,** change the **f** or **fe** to **v** before adding **es** to make the word plural, or mean more than one.

wolf   wolv**es**   knife   kniv**es**

Read each word listed below. Add the ending **s** or **es** to each word to make it plural, or mean more than one. Then write the word on the line.

1. calf   calves   2. leaf   _____

3. loaf   _____   4. stove   _____

5. yard   _____   6. wife   _____

7. elf   _____   8. team   _____

9. shadow   _____   10. shelf   _____

11. life   _____   12. bank   _____

13. scarf   _____   14. half   _____

15. thief   _____   16. wharf   _____

17. cartoon   _____   18. yourself   _____

19. self   _____   20. stamp   _____

To show that an object belongs to one person or thing, add **'s** to the end of the word.

 dog bone =  dog**'s** bone

Look at the first two pictures. Read the words next to them. Then look at the last picture and add ' to the first word next to the picture to show that something belongs to it.

1. dentist   drill   dentist **'s** drill

2. pilot   plane   pilot___ plane

3. school   flag   school___ flag

4. Mary   bike   Mary___ bike

5. baby   crib   baby___ crib

6. Nick   jacket   Nick___ jacket

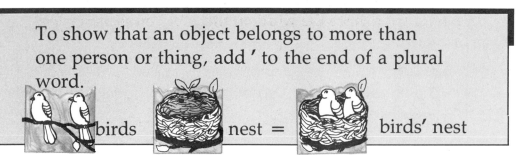

To show that an object belongs to more than one person or thing, add ' to the end of a plural word.

birds + nest = birds' nest

Look at the first two pictures. Read the words next to them. Then look at the last picture and add ' to the first word next to the picture to show that something belongs to it.

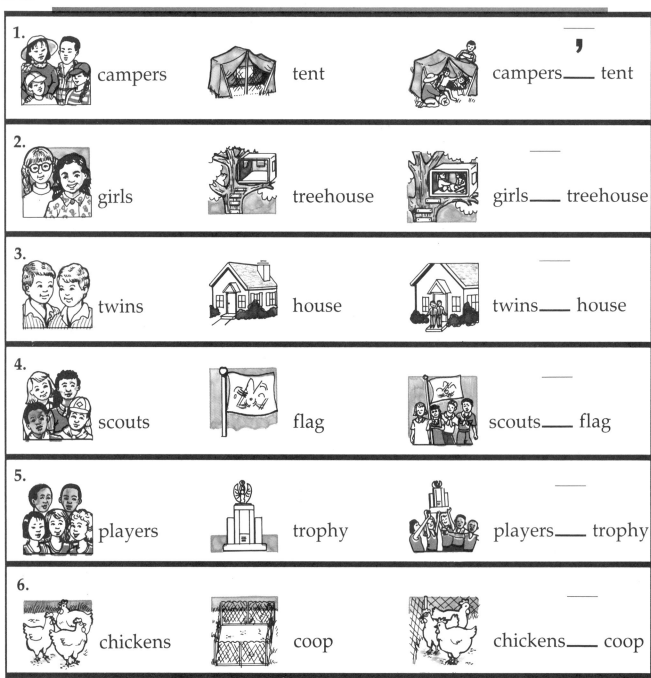

1. campers   tent   campers__ tent

2. girls   treehouse   girls__ treehouse

3. twins   house   twins__ house

4. scouts   flag   scouts__ flag

5. players   trophy   players__ trophy

6. chickens   coop   chickens__ coop

NAME _____

Read each sentence. Add the ending **s** or **es** to make a word plural, or mean more than one. Then write the word on the line. You may need to make spelling changes.

1. We have four soup bowls but not enough flat ___dishes___. **dish**

2. Mom and Dad pay their _____ every April.   **tax**

3. The bus stops before it _____ train tracks.   **pass**

4. Sal has four blue _____ in his shirt pocket.   **pencil**

5. Dad painted all the doors and _____ bright red.   **shelf**

6. The fire chief told us never to play with _____.   **match**

7. I like to read about the _____ of famous people.   **life**

8. When you split a melon, you have two _____.   **half**

9. Mom keeps three sharp _____ in the locked drawer.   **knife**

10. All the children rode their _____ to the park.   **bike**

11. My _____ won prizes at the county fair.   **calf**

12. You will find a dozen water _____ in the carton.   **glass**

13. Did you hear the hungry _____ howling last night?   **wolf**

14. There are colorful _____ in my quilt.   **patch**

Look at each picture. Then read the sentence. Circle the word that completes the sentence. Then write the word on the line.

	1. That __deer's__ horns are huge.	(deer's) deers'
	2. The _____ lunchroom is busy.	student's students'
	3. _____ is studying for a test.	Ron Ron's
	4. The _____ lockers are over there.	girl's girls'
	5. The _____ dens are under the rocks.	snake's snakes'
	6. _____ bat is in her locker.	Jan Jan's
	7. My _____ mitt is too tight for Carla.	catcher's catchers'
	8. Those _____ ships are at the dock.	sailor's sailors'

REVIEW Singular and plural possessive forms

A suffix is a word part that is added to the end of a word. It changes the meaning of the word.

The suffix **ful** means **full of.**
The suffix **less** means **without.**

care + ful = careful   care + less = careless

Look at each picture. Then add the suffix **ful** or **less** to the word next to the picture.

1. help less   help _____

2. color _____   color _____

3. use _____   use _____

4. power _____   power _____

5. thought _____   thought _____

6. fear _____   fear _____

7. pain _____   pain _____

Read each sentence. Add the suffix **ful** or **less** to each word to
complete the sentence. Then write the word on the line.

1. Mike will get cut if he is __careless__ with that knife. **care**

2. Please be _____ when crossing the street. **care**

3. A sprained ankle can be very _____. **pain**

4. An eye exam is usually _____. **pain**

5. The person who pushed me in the hall is _____. **thought**

6. Rosa was _____ when she sent me a get-well card. **thought**

7. A kitten is _____ and needs care. **help**

8. Pete cooks and is always _____ around the house. **help**

9. When you want to paint, an easel is _____. **use**

10. Broken cups and cracked plates are _____. **use**

11. The pretty flowers make the garden very _____. **color**

12. Before the blank wall was painted, it was _____. **color**

13. The cat is _____ without its claws. **power**

14. A huge steam shovel is very _____. **power**

Suffixes **ful** and **less**

A suffix is a word part that is added to the end of a word. It changes the meaning of the word.

The suffix **er** can mean **a person who**
The suffix **ness** can mean **condition or state.**

paint + er = painter   a person who paints

sad + ness = sadness   the state of being sad

Look at each picture. Read the word next to the picture. Add the suffix **er** or **ness** to the word. Then write the word on the line. You may need to make spelling changes.

1. drive __driver__

2. soft _____

3. loud _____

4. catch _____

5. dance _____

6. skate _____

7. dry _____

8. bright _____

9. clumsy _____

10. drum _____

11. ride _____

12. run _____

13. thick _____

14. dark _____

Read each sentence. Add the suffix **er** or **ness** to each word to
complete the sentence. Then write the word on the line. You may
need to make spelling changes.

1. Look at the **thickness** of her egg salad sandwich! **thick**

2. The _____ of the music makes it hard to hear you. **loud**

3. Our bus _____ knows all the streets in town. **drive**

4. We all laughed at the clown's _____. **clumsy**

5. Kim will be a ballet _____ one day. **dance**

6. My brother likes horses and is a great _____. **ride**

7. The _____ of the soil caused the plants to die. **dry**

8. Clara is the newest _____ on our team. **catch**

9. The _____ of the flashing lights blinded me. **bright**

10. I like to feel the _____ of a rabbit's fur. **soft**

11. Dad said that someday I'll be a fast _____. **run**

12. Jacob is the most graceful _____ in the show. **skate**

13. Turn off all the lights and you will be in _____. **dark**

14. The _____ in the school band is my sister. **drum**

A suffix is a word part that is added to the end of a word. It changes the meaning of the word.

The suffix **y** can mean **having** or **full of.**
The suffix **ly** can mean **in a certain way.**

dirt + y = dirty full of dirt

quick + ly = quickly in a quick way

Look at each picture. Read the word next to the picture. Add the suffix **y** or **ly** to the word. Then write the word on the line.

1. wind _windy_	2. neat _____
3. correct _____	4. wrong _____
5. curl _____	6. bump _____
7. tight _____	8. complete _____
9. leak _____	10. free _____
11. thirst _____	12. snow _____
13. cream _____	14. slow _____

Read each sentence. Add the suffix **y** or **ly** to each word to complete
the sentence. Then write the word on the line.

1. A taxi driver must be careful on a __snowy__ day. **snow**

2. The flag is flying _____ in the wind. **free**

3. I get very _____ on hot summer days. **thirst**

4. Ed holds my hand _____ when crossing a street. **tight**

5. The salad dressing is thick and _____. **cream**

6. The _____ boat started to sink in the water. **leak**

7. Brenda's hair is as _____ as her father's. **curl**

8. Look at the turtle crawling _____ across the yard. **slow**

9. Sid _____ joined the winner's circle. **glad**

10. On _____ days the sky is full of colorful kites. **wind**

11. Teresa is always _____ dressed. **neat**

12. Lisa's house is on a winding and _____ street. **bump**

13. If you come with us, you have to walk _____. **quick**

14. The sky is _____ filled with big dark clouds. **complete**

Read each meaning below. Add the suffix **ful, less, er, ness, y,** or **ly** to each word shown in heavy type. Then write the word on the line. You may need to make spelling changes.

1.	one who **catches** catcher	2.	in a **quick** way
3.	full of **wind**	4.	full of **help**
5.	without **fear**	6.	in a **neat** way
7.	being **clumsy**	8.	full of **snow**
9.	full of **pain**	10.	one who **runs**
11.	without **thought**	12.	being **dark**
13.	one who **flies**	14.	full of **thought**
15.	being **bright**	16.	without **power**
17.	full of **salt**	18.	in a **sudden** way

Read each sentence. Add the suffix **ful, less, er, ness, y,** or **ly** to each word. Then write the word on the line. You may need to make spelling changes.

1. City buses have powerful engines. **power**

2. Tasha was _____ when she forgot to call us. **thought**

3. The _____ used bright colors on the walls. **paint**

4. There was much _____ when we lost the last game. **sad**

5. Lisa is always _____ after a game of baseball. **thirst**

6. Did I do the test _____? **correct**

7. Mom drove the car slowly down the _____ hill. **bump**

8. A pencil without a sharp point is _____. **use**

9. Dad is a _____ and Mom is a runner. **skate**

10. When riding her bike, Alison is always very _____. **care**

11. I like the velvety _____ of the new carpet. **soft**

12. I want to study music so I can become a _____. **drum**

13. My clothes get _____ when I play in the mud. **dirt**

14. Last night rain came through the _____ roof. **leak**

REVIEW Suffixes **ful, less, er, ness, y,** and **ly**

Read each word listed below. Circle the suffix to show that the suffix forms a syllable. Then on the line write the number of syllables that are left in the base word.

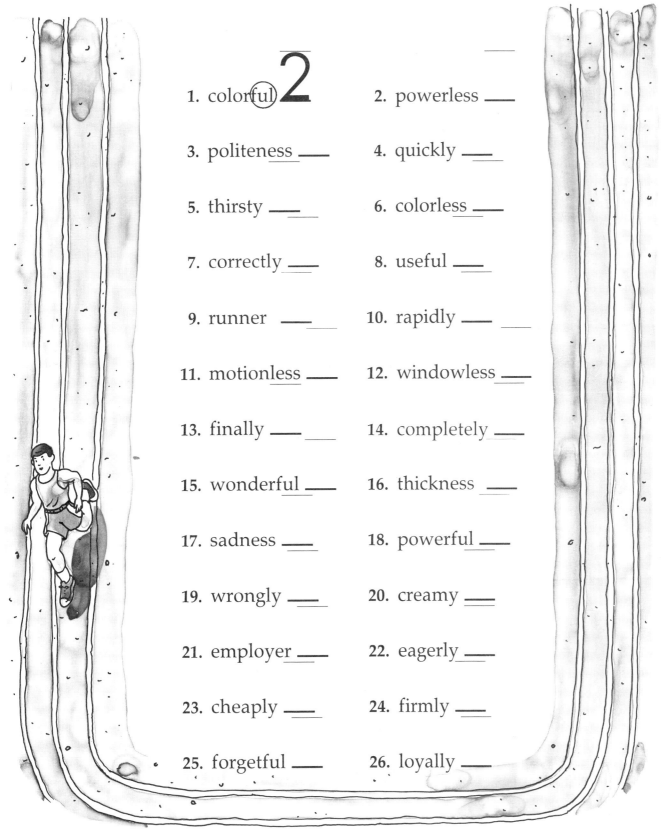

1. color(ful) 2

2. powerless ___

3. politeness ___

4. quickly ___

5. thirsty ___

6. colorless ___

7. correctly ___

8. useful ___

9. runner ___

10. rapidly ___

11. motionless ___

12. windowless ___

13. finally ___

14. completely ___

15. wonderful ___

16. thickness ___

17. sadness ___

18. powerful ___

19. wrongly ___

20. creamy ___

21. employer ___

22. eagerly ___

23. cheaply ___

24. firmly ___

25. forgetful ___

26. loyally ___

Read each word listed below. Draw a line between the syllables in each word.

1. help/ful
2. thickness
3. silently
4. neatly
5. snowy
6. careless
7. dreamer
8. painful
9. joyful
10. shadowy
11. darkness
12. openly
13. eagerness
14. starter
15. lemony
16. catcher
17. rapidly
18. thankful
19. painter
20. sleepy
21. brightness
22. slowly
23. stainless
24. cleverly
25. traveler
26. windy
27. suddenly
28. correctly
29. velvety
30. freely

NAME _____

Read each sentence. Circle the word that completes the sentence. Then write the word on the line.

_____

1. Look at the _____ splashing around in the pond. **beavers** **beaver's**

2. The _____ van is parked in our driveway. **movers** **movers'**

3. Dave uses two _____ to polish the school floors. **waxes** **wax's**

4. The fire _____ left front tire is flat. **trucks** **truck's**

5. The _____ camp was far from the nearest town. **armies** **army's**

6. How many _____ do you ride to school each day? **buses** **bus's**

7. The girls wore their yellow _____ on Sunday. **dresses** **dress's**

8. The _____ howling scared the children. **wolves** **wolf's**

9. I helped Dad cut the grass and plant rose _____. **bushes** **bush's**

10. My _____ sleeve is still ripped. **coats** **coat's**

11. We found the _____ hive in our backyard. **bees** **bees'**

12. Pat ate two thick ham _____. **sandwiches** **sandwich's**

13. Grandpa always goes to the woods to pick _____. **berries** **berry's**

14. The _____ meeting is Tuesday morning. **clubs** **club's**

Add the ending to each word listed below. Then write the word on the line. You may need to make spelling changes.

1. close + est _____   2. skate + ing _____

3. vote + ing _____   4. dance + ed _____

5. hot + er _____   6. thin + est _____

7. clap + ed _____   8. knot + ing _____

9. blue + er _____   10. short + est _____

Complete each sentence by choosing a word from above. Write the word on the line.

_____

1. We all _____ our hands at the end of the magic show.

2. Sailors on deck were _____ the ship's ropes.

3. The sand at the beach is _____ on a sunny day.

4. This is the _____ slice of cake I ever saw!

5. José sang and _____ in the show.

6. The children are _____ on the frozen pond.

7. Tim's shirt is _____ than mine.

8. February is the _____ month of the year.

Add the ending to each word listed below. Write the word on the line.
You may need to make spelling changes.

1. cry + ed _____

2. penny + es _____

3. elf + es _____

4. silly + est _____

5. monkey + s _____

6. hurry + ed _____

7. scarf + es _____

8. happy + est _____

9. early + er _____

10. city + es _____

Complete each sentence by choosing a word from above. Write the
word on the line.

1. Angela gave me _____ and dimes for my bank.

2. I _____ when I fell and hit my head on the ice.

3. Dad gets up _____ than Mom every morning.

4. The _____ in the play wore green caps and shoes.

5. There are lots of people and traffic in _____.

6. We _____ to the airport so we would not miss our plane.

7. Our _____ just came back from the cleaners.

8. The _____ at the zoo are cute and playful.

Read each sentence. Circle the word that completes the sentence. Then write the word on the line.

1. Bianca took a _____ of honey for her sore throat. **spoon**
   spoonful

2. The long freight train seemed _____. **end**
   endless

3. Our letter _____ is late with today's mail. **carry**
   carrier

4. When I was _____, I missed a week of school. **sick**
   sickness

5. We were _____ to find the lost books. **luck**
   lucky

6. Ted is _____ when diving into the swimming pool. **care**
   careful

7. Sandy was _____ when she entered the contest. **hope**
   hopeful

8. A car without a motor is _____. **power**
   powerless

9. Sam got one _____ in today's game. **hit**
   hitter

10. Winning the gold medal caused great _____. **happy**
    happiness

11. Today is a wet and _____ day. **rain**
    rainy

12. The sun shone _____ after the snow storm. **bright**
    brightly

13. It's _____ in the shade. **chill**
    chilly

14. The _____ thunder scared the puppy. **loud**
    loudness

TEST Inflectional endings and suffixes

A prefix is a word part that is added to the beginning of a word. It changes the meaning of the word.

The prefix **un** means **not**, or **opposite of**.
The prefix **re** means **again**, or **do over**.

un + wrap = unwrap   re + wrap = rewrap

Read the words listed below. Then look at the pictures. Add the prefix **un** or **re** to the word and write the new word on the line.

1.
lock   unlock   _____

2.
tie   _____   _____

3.
load   _____   _____

4.
wind   _____   _____

5.
fold   _____   _____

6.
pack   _____   _____

Read each pair of sentences. Add the prefix **un** or **re** to the word to
complete each sentence. Then write the new word on the line.

1. When Lisa arrives, she will ___**unpack**___ her suitcase.

   When Lisa leaves, she will _____ her suitcase. **pack**

2. Please _____ the box so I can see what is in it.

   Now you may _____ the box so it can be mailed. **wrap**

3. Let us _____ the blanket and put it on the bed.

   Later we will _____ the blanket and put it away. **fold**

4. Craig must _____ the rope to make a clothesline.

   He will _____ all the rope he doesn't use. **wind**

5. Jay must _____ the laces to take off his shoes.

   To wear his shoes again, he must _____ the laces. **tie**

6. Daniel has to _____ the gate to get into the yard.

   When Daniel leaves, he will _____ the gate. **lock**

7. The workers have come to _____ crates of fruit.

   Later they will _____ the van with the empty crates. **load**

A prefix is a word part that is added to the
beginning of a word. It changes the meaning
of the word.

The prefix **dis** means **not,** or **opposite of**.

dis + honest = dishonest

Look at each picture. Read the word next to the picture. Add the
prefix **dis** to the word. Then write the word on the line.

1. like **dislike**	**2.** connect _____
3. approve _____	**4.** agree _____
5. appear _____	**6.** locate _____
7. please _____	**8.** order _____
9. infect _____	**10.** obey _____
11. comfort _____	**12.** mount _____

Read each sentence. Use meaning clues to choose the word that completes the sentence. Circle that word. Then write the word on the line.

1. Kevin and Anna like grapes, but they __dislike__ apples.   like (dislike)

2. Are you ready to _____ and ride your horse?   mount **dismount**

3. Mia didn't _____ the TV before the storm.   connect **disconnect**

4. I think you are correct, so I _____ with you.   agree **disagree**

5. Cyrus left his cluttered room in _____.   order **disorder**

6. The sun will _____ as the clouds go away.   appear **disappear**

7. Careful drivers _____ traffic signals.   obey **disobey**

8. After the long ride, Bob was happy to _____.   mount **dismount**

9. We _____ our coach when we play our best.   please **displease**

10. Tooth decay often causes _____.   comfort **discomfort**

11. A pitcher can very easily _____ a shoulder.   locate **dislocate**

12. I am happy my parents _____ of studying drums.   approve **disapprove**

13. The bright sun will _____ the curtains.   color **discolor**

14. Germs can _____ you and make you sick.   infect **disinfect**

Read each meaning below. Add the prefix **un, re,** or **dis** to each word shown in heavy type. Then write the new word on the line.

1. opposite of **load**	2. pack **again**
unload	
3. opposite of **lock**	4. opposite of **comfort**
5. opposite of **please**	6. **tie** again
7. opposite of **agree**	8. opposite of **fold**
9. opposite of **approve**	10. opposite of **appear**
11. **tell** again	12. opposite of **order**
13. opposite of **do**	14. **wrap** again
15. opposite of **button**	16. **seal** again
17. not **true**	18. **build** again

Read each sentence. Add the prefix **un, re,** or **dis** to each word to
complete the sentence. Then write the new word on the line.

1. We have to __unfold__ the sheets before we make the bed. **fold**

2. Too much sunshine will _____ the green carpet. **color**

3. Anita will _____ the cartons of books. **pack**

4. Lucas helped me _____ the package you mailed to me. **wrap**

5. Bob will _____ the door so I can get into the car. **lock**

6. Sometimes Leah will _____ with her sister's ideas. **agree**

7. Sam had to _____ his shoelace so he wouldn't trip. **tie**

8. My friends Todd and Jay _____ flying in planes. **like**

9. Tight fitting shoes can cause _____. **comfort**

10. Joan will _____ her suitcase so everything fits. **pack**

11. Did you _____ the door after you came home? **lock**

12. The books on the second shelf are in _____. **order**

13. I will _____ Mother if I don't eat my supper. **please**

14. We had to _____ the towels that fell off the shelf. **fold**

Read each word listed below. Circle the prefix to show that the prefix forms a syllable. Then on the line write the number of syllables that are left in the base word.

1. (un)pack ____

2. disappear ____

3. dismount ____

4. retie ____

5. refold ____

6. disobey ____

7. disconnect ____

8. dislike ____

9. discolor ____

10. unwind ____

11. unfold ____

12. displease ____

13. rewind ____

14. unlock ____

15. dislocate ____

16. disorder ____

17. unload ____

18. discomfort ____

19. untie ____

20. reload ____

21. disagree ____

22. rewrap ____

23. relock ____

24. disapprove ____

25. disinfect ____

26. repack ____

Read each sentence. Circle the word that completes the sentence. Then write the word on the line.

1. Adam and Brad _____ Ms. Jones when they are late.   **please**
  displease

2. When a clock stops ticking, you have to _____ it.   **unwind**
  rewind

3. Let's _____ the gift so we can see what's in it.   **unwrap**
  rewrap

4. _____ the radio by pulling out the plug.   **Connect**
  Disconnect

5. Tony will _____ his napkin and put it on his lap.   **unfold**
  refold

6. Mom will _____ the shed so we can get the rake.   **unlock**
  relock

7. If Kim falls on the ice, she could _____ her hip.   **locate**
  dislocate

8. Please _____ your sweater so it fits in the drawer.   **unfold**
  refold

9. Dad will _____ the car trunk so everything fits.   **unpack**
  repack

10. That answer is wrong and I _____ with it.   **agree**
  disagree

11. After my ride, I happily _____ from my horse.   **mount**
  dismount

12. Alan cannot _____ his knotted scarf.   **untie**
  retie

13. Lazy people _____ hard work.   **like**
  dislike

14. The workers will _____ the van with the cartons.   **unload**
  reload

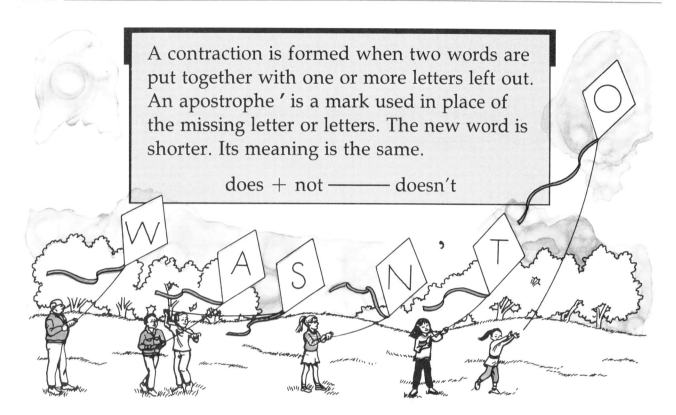

A contraction is formed when two words are put together with one or more letters left out. An apostrophe ' is a mark used in place of the missing letter or letters. The new word is shorter. Its meaning is the same.

does + not ——— doesn't

In each box draw a line from each pair of words to the contraction the words form.

1.
was + not   haven't
have + not   hasn't
has + not   wasn't

2.
were + not   don't
do + not   can't
can + not   weren't

3.
are + not   didn't
is + not   hadn't
had + not   isn't
did + not   aren't

4.
could + not   wouldn't
would + not   shouldn't
should + not   musn't
must + not   couldn't

5.
she + is   it's
it + is   who's
what + is   what's
who + is   she's

6.
there + is   that's
he + is   where's
where + is   he's
that + is   there's

Contraction **n't** and **'s**   Unit 12/Lesson 85   **207**

Read each sentence. Put the words together to form a contraction.
Then write the contraction on the line.

1. "I hope we **aren't** late for school," said Luis. (are + not)

2. Look! _____ not a cloud in the sky. (There + is)

3. _____ that your sister I saw in the bookstore? (Was + not)

4. Linda _____ get to her music lesson on time. (could + not)

5. _____ the key to unlock the toy chest? (Where + is)

6. Ken _____ mow the lawn or trim the trees. (did + not)

7. I know _____ my baseball bat. (that + is)

8. _____ it time for lunch yet? (Is + not)

9. Sarah _____ like to jog or swim. (does + not)

10. _____ trying out for a part in the play? (Who + is)

11. I _____ done my math problems yet. (have + not)

12. We _____ caught in the traffic jam last night. (were + not)

13. _____ the longest river in the world? (What + is)

14. My plants _____ be watered too often. (must + not)

Contractions n't and 's

A contraction is formed when two words are put together with one or more letters left out. An apostrophe ' is a mark used in place of the missing letter or letters. The new word is shorter. Its meaning is the same.

you + will ———— you'll

In each box draw a line from each pair of words to the contraction the words form.

1.
we + will ————we'll
he + will   it'll
it + will   he'll

2.
I + will   she'll
she + will   they'll
they + will   I'll

3.
they + would   she'd
she + would   I'd
I + would   they'd

4.
we + would   you'd
he + would   we'd
you + would   who'd
who + would   he'd

Read each sentence. Put the words together to form a contraction.
Then write the contraction on the line.

1. I just know ___**it'll**___ be sunny when we go sailing. (it + will)

2. _____ help you move the chairs into the hall. (They + will)

3. Ask Daniel if _____ pack the boxes for us. (he + will)

4. _____ have gone hiking if it were a sunny day. (We + would)

5. Carlos said _____ like to play shortstop. (he + would)

6. _____ like to go with us to the skating rink. (They + would)

7. We are sure that _____ be there on time. (she + will)

8. _____ be surprised to see how tall I have grown. (You + will)

9. Now here's what _____ do! (we + will)

10. _____ enjoy reading my new book. (She + would)

11. _____ put all our games on the closet shelf. (We + will)

12. _____ see if the doctor is in her office. (I + will)

13. Did Mom know _____ be late for supper? (you + would)

14. _____ like to learn about whales and robots. (I + would)

Contractions 'll and 'd

Read the words listed below. Put the words together to form a
contraction. Then write the contraction on the line.

1. she + is __she's__

2. I + would _____

3. was + not _____

4. could + not _____

5. can + not _____

6. there + is _____

7. he + is _____

8. did + not _____

9. were + not _____

10. we + will _____

11. it + is _____

12. they + will _____

13. they + would _____

14. is + not _____

15. you + will _____

16. has + not _____

17. she + would _____

18. I + will _____

19. who + is _____

20. would + not _____

21. you + would _____

22. it + will _____

23. we + would _____

24. that + is _____

25. are + not _____

26. what + is _____

27. must + not _____

28. should + not _____

Read each sentence. Put the words together to form a contraction.
Then write the contraction on the line.

1. **We'd** _____ like to sing a new song for you. (**We + would**)

2. Luis and Kim _____ found the paint brushes. (**have + not**)

3. Diedre will go to the parade if _____ go too. (**you + will**)

4. Do you think _____ ready to go home? (**he + is**)

5. _____ my turn to water the plants. (**It + is**)

6. Adam _____ want to play his trumpet. (**does + not**)

7. The squirrels knew _____ have nuts for them. (**you + would**)

8. I think _____ read a good story. (**I + will**)

9. I wonder _____ want those old skates. (**who + would**)

10. Rachel hopes _____ like her new puppet show. (**they + will**)

11. Anna and John _____ wait for me. (**would + not**)

12. _____ the pony I like to ride! (**There + is**)

13. Hurry! _____ be late for the race. (**We + will**)

14. We _____ all work on the play after school. (**can + not**)

A contraction is formed when two words are put together with one or more letters left out. An apostrophe ' is a mark used in place of the missing letter or letters. The new word is shorter. Its meaning is the same.

I + am —— I'm   they + have —— they've

In each box draw a line from each pair of words to the contraction the words form.

1.
you are	I'm
they have	you're
I am	they've

2.
we are	let's
they are	we're
let us	they're

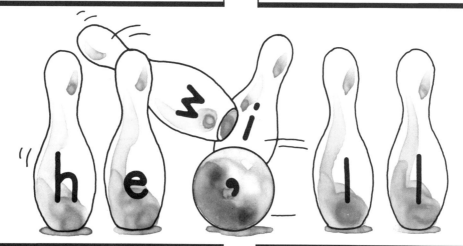

3.
we have	he'll
I would	you've
you have	we've
he will	I'd

4.
they will	I've
he would	they'll
I have	shouldn't
should not	he'd

Read each sentence. Put the words together to form a contraction.
Then write the contraction on the line.

1. 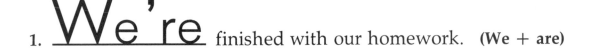 **We're** finished with our homework. (We + are)

2. _____ my very best friend! (You + are)

3. _____ afraid the box will not fit in the closet. (I + am)

4. _____ going to hike the steep trail up the mountain. (They + are)

5. Can you guess how many stories _____ read today? (I + have)

6. _____ a very colorful shirt on today. (You + have)

7. _____ have some of those ripe red cherries. (Let + us)

8. I think _____ just finished their lunch. (they + have)

9. _____ been to the new playground four times. (We + have)

10. _____ both go fishing next Saturday morning. (Let + us)

11. José said _____ ready to start the movie. (they + are)

12. _____ won our last six soccer games. (We + have)

13. _____ always wanted to ride a camel. (I + have)

14. _____ a new member of the baseball team. (I + am)

Read the words listed below. Put the words together to form a
contraction. Then write the contraction on the line.

1. I + am _____ I'm _____

2. we + will _____

3. you + have _____

4. she + would _____

5. we + are _____

6. it + will _____

7. they + are _____

8. what + is _____

9. I + have _____

10. you + will _____

11. you + are _____

12. we + have _____

13. I + will _____

14. who + is _____

15. we + would _____

16. they + would _____

17. have + not _____

18. let + us _____

19. they + have _____

20. where + is _____

21. are + not _____

22. she + is _____

23. I + would _____

24. he + will _____

25. can + not _____

26. could + not _____

27. he + would _____

28. had + not _____

Read each sentence. Put the words together to form a contraction.
Then write the contraction on the line.

1. We _____ ready for the next game. (are + not)

2. _____ the largest city in the world? (What + is)

3. It _____ be wise to leave before the storm. (would + not)

4. _____ come earlier to set up chairs. (They + will)

5. _____ going to be a graceful dancer. (You + are)

6. _____ starting a stamp collection. (I + am)

7. _____ going to have cheese sandwiches. (We + are)

8. I know _____ playing with my jump rope. (she + is)

9. _____ going to catch that thief? (Who + is)

10. Do you know _____ the biggest wagon? (we + have)

11. _____ do the dishes before we play. (Let + us)

12. Dave _____ go out until Mom comes. (can + not)

13. _____ a very painful sore throat. (I + have)

14. _____ like to plan a picnic in the woods. (They + would)

TEST Contractions n't, 'll, 'd, 'm, 're, 've, and 's

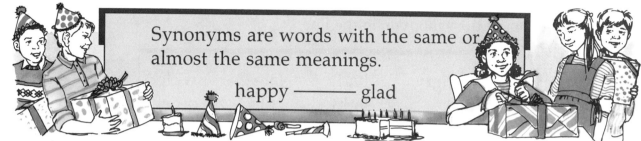

Synonyms are words with the same or almost the same meanings.

happy —— glad

Draw a line between the synonyms, or words that have the same meaning.

1.

cold — chilly
angry   mad
loud   little
small   late
tardy   noisy

2.

fast   tall
high   quick
buy   finish
wet   soaked
end   purchase

Choose a synonym from the box for the underlined word. Then write the word on the line.

1. a <u>bright</u> smile   a **cheerful** smile

2. ready to <u>go</u>   ready to _____

3. the <u>last</u> question   the _____ question

4. a <u>bad</u> choice   a _____ choice

5. play <u>indoors</u>   play _____

6. a <u>quiet</u> room   a _____ room

7. a <u>big</u> fire truck   a _____ fire truck

cheerful

wrong

leave

silent

inside

final

large

Select a synonym from the box below for the word after each sentence. Then write the synonym on the line.

hungry	bad	late	wide
fast	light	cold	quiet
strong	shut	hard	

1. Don is wearing a  blue shirt. **pale**

2. It is _____ out on the porch. **chilly**

3. The giant had _____ arms. **powerful**

4. The children were _____ after the games. **starved**

5. A _____ train took us to the city. **swift**

6. Please _____ the door when you leave the room. **close**

7. Mr. Hill doesn't like his pupils to be _____. **tardy**

8. The red hat had a _____ brim. **broad**

9. Pam lost the game with a _____ move. **wrong**

10. The clay turned _____ during the night. **firm**

11. In the country everything is so _____. **peaceful**

Synonyms

Antonyms are words that are opposite in meaning.

first ——— last

Draw a line between **two words** that have the opposite meaning.

1.

fast   go
come   slow
cold   climb
before   hot
fall   after

2.

back   less
best   low
empty   full
high   worst
more   front

Choose an antonym from the box for the underlined word. Then write the word on the line.

1. up the hill   **down** the hill

2. to lose my dog   to _____ my dog

3. the old store   the _____ store

4. open the door   _____ the door

5. in the summer   in the _____

6. the last bus stop   the _____ bus stop

7. the best picture   the _____ picture

find

close

down

worst

winter

first

new

Read the words in the box. Then answer each riddle by writing on the line the word from the box that is an antonym for the underlined word.

light	front	right	above
stand	cool	lose	fat

1. I am an antonym for <u>sit</u> and I have five letters. What word am I? __stand__

2. I have four letters. I mean the opposite of <u>win</u>. I am _____.

3. I am an antonym for <u>left</u> and I have five letters. What word am I? _____

4. I have five letters. I mean the opposite of <u>heavy</u>. I am _____.

5. I am an antonym for <u>below</u> and I have five letters. What word am I? _____

6. I have three letters. I mean the opposite of <u>thin</u>. I am _____.

7. I am an antonym for <u>warm</u> and I have four letters. What word am I? _____

8. I have five letters. I mean the opposite of <u>back</u>. I am _____.

Homonyms are words that sound the same.
They have different meanings.

pear ——— pair

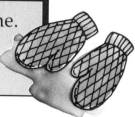

Draw a line between two words that have the same sound.

1.

bear ——————— bare
flour   pale
made   flower
road   maid
pail   rode

2.

blue   whole
eye   two
hole   blew
sea   see
to   I

Choose a homonym for the underlined word. Then write the word on the line.

1. buy a dress   _____ by _____ my side

2. to write a letter   my _____ hand

3. a long tail   to tell a _____

4. hear a noise   come _____

5. eat a roll   play a _____

6. through the tunnel   _____ the ball

7. in one week   a _____ person

here

role

weak

by

tale

right

threw

Homonyms

Read the clues for the crossword puzzle. Choose a homonym for each clue from the box. Then use the homonym to complete the puzzle.

threw	would	for	son	plane	pail
beet	eye	tail	ate	weak	flower
write	hear	heel	road	sale	no
meat	in	mail	roll	hole	sent

Across

1. cent
3. pale
4. inn
7. flour
9. male
10. here
12. through
15. right
17. sun
18. wood
19. meet
20. heal

Down

1. sail
2. tale
3. plain
5. know
6. beat
7. four
8. I
11. eight
13. role
14. rode
15. week
16. whole

Homonyms

Read the clues for the crossword puzzle. Choose a synonym, antonym, or homonym for each clue from the box. Write the word to complete the puzzle.

sit	out	close	down	wrong	son
cent	end	maid	strong	right	winter
mad	sad	stop	loud	sail	through

Across

2. bad
3. sun
5. angry
6. write
8. finish
11. in
13. powerful
14. stand

Down

1. up
2. summer
3. happy
4. open
5. made
7. threw
9. sent
10. start
12. noisy
13. sale

For each pair of words, write **S** if the words are synonyms, **A** if they are antonyms, and **H** if they are homonyms.

1. high   tall   _____   15. son   sun   _____

2. heavy   light   _____   16. back   front   _____

3. blue   blew   _____   17. young   old   _____

4. sale   sail   _____   18. would   wood   _____

5. angry   mad   _____   19. indoors inside   _____

6. pail   pale   _____   20. empty   full   _____

7. hungry   starved   _____   21. wide   broad   _____

8. fast   slow   _____   22. pale   light   _____

9. roll   role   _____   23. best   worst   _____

10. powerful   strong   _____   24. cold   chilly   _____

11. fat   thin   _____   25. open   close   _____

12. loud   noisy   _____   26. warm   cool   _____

13. sit   stand   _____   27. threw   through   _____

14. week   weak   _____   28. hear   here   _____